WRITING FOR UNDERSTANDING:

Using Backward Design to Help
All Students Write Effectively

THE VERMONT WRITING COLLABORATIVE:

JOEY HAWKINS

ELOISE GINTY

KAREN LECLAIRE KURZMAN

DIANA LEDDY

JANE MILLER

Published by:
Vermont Writing Collaborative
PO Box 156
South Strafford, VT 05070
phone: (802) 765-4040
joeylornell@gmail.com

Cover Design: Kiet Randolph, *www.randolphdesignhaus.com*
Interior Design and Typesetting: 1106 Design, *www.1106design.com*

Printed in the United States of America.

Table of Contents

Dedication

We dedicate our work to our students,
and to all students—it is for you,
and because of you,
that we have written this book.

Foreword

"Some people think I'm only interested in voice or feelings,
but I'm interested in hard thinking, so I push for hard
thinking, too…. When I give feedback to students, I often
talk about issues of voice, but almost always I'm trying to
get the thinking to be stronger."

—Peter Elbow

http://www.etext.org/Zines/Critique/writing/elbow.html

You would think that I would be a big fan of the writing process. After all, I am a published author, a former teacher of English, and a firm believer in the need to focus on learning how to learn. But I am not a fan. I have always wondered how it is that "the process," as taught in classrooms across the country, bears little resemblance to the approaches I use to accomplish my best writing. And in my experience, it speaks little to the two hardest parts of writing: thinking things deeply, all the way through; and revising to meet the audience's high standards.

Writing is "hard thinking" (as Elbow puts it, above), and thinking one's ideas all the way through, until they are clear not only to the writer herself but also to others, is a great challenge for all writers. What am I trying to say? What has not been said before?

How might I help my readers see or feel in a new way? Lying awake, agitated by such questions, is the gauntlet all would-be writers must run. Such hard thinking is essential to writing that would make readers respond with their own new thoughts and feelings.

Yet, while necessary, such intensity of thought is not sufficient. A writer can think till it hurts, but if she doesn't really understand her subject from the inside out, she won't have much to offer a reader. The authors of *Writing for Understanding* remind us throughout this thorough and practical book that the best writing depends upon clear and vital ideas about a subject - not simply practiced skill in stringing pretty sentences together. As the authors so succinctly put it, "Many problems in writing are really problems in understanding: students often know little about what they are trying to write."

What's the point of a process if, as a writer, you have nothing significant to say? And how can you have something significant to say if you lack sufficient expertise about or hard-won insight into your topic? The chief contribution of this book's authors lies in a deceptively simple but easily overlooked idea: a plan for ensuring that disciplined inquiry into the "content" of the writing must be made a crucial part of writing instruction and the writing experience.

Knowledge about the topic is only part of the understanding needed, however. You may know your topic, but what about understanding excellent writing? The authors astutely emphasize the use of models as a key in helping learners understand good writing by focusing constantly on the end result—excellent writing. The most important issue is not what excellent writers "do," but what excellent writers "accomplish." We need to study their accomplishments more than their processes, extracting useful inferences about what good writing is, then transferring those to our own writing. The authors of *Writing for Understanding* thus propose an approach that does not abandon the writing process but, instead, extends and refocuses it, integrating method with a persistent concern about product – "backward design" from excellent writing, rather than process alone.

This focus on product yields results. A few years ago, in a district in Ohio, the fourth grade was divided into two groups. One half of the students was taught the writing process and followed it for each writing assignment. The other half received no exposure to the writing process. Instead, before each assignment, the students read, analyzed, and discussed a variety of models of writing. The latter group significantly outperformed the former group on the state writing test. As the Vermont Writing Collaborative points out, there is only one way to understand excellence and that is to study it, then work to emulate it. That effort requires models, many of them, as well as an analysis by students, led by teachers, of those models.

What's the practical value of the authors' approach? Students become clearer in their knowledge and their expression, and their increased success leads to increased confidence. As the authors note, in describing the outcome of their work with developing writers, "Students by and large know what they are doing. They know how to proceed with a focused, organized, thoughtful plan for their writing. It is a rare child who says, 'I don't know what to do', or 'I don't have anything to say about this.'" That is a happy result, indeed, and one that can be too rare in our classrooms. This book demonstrates, in clear detail and with multiple examples, how to help students come to expect to make meaning in their writing, how to recognize the qualities of excellent writing, and how to work, incrementally, to achieve such excellence themselves.

Writing will always be difficult—it remains so to me after twenty-five years of writing professionally. But what the Vermont Writing Collaborative has done is provide a fresh, comprehensive yet practical strategy for making good writing seem more attainable—a lesson the young writer who struggles to write well needs so badly to learn as early as possible.

—Grant Wiggins

Preface
Writing for Understanding and the
Common Core Standards:
What's the Connection?

In 2010, Common Core State Standards (CCSS) for English Language Arts and Literacy, as well as Mathematics, were released to the public. Initiated by the Council of Chief State School Officers and the National Governors' Association and extensively reviewed by states, the Standards were created to raise the rigor of what is expected from students and teachers in a consistent way across the states. In the words of the Common Core, these standards attempt to "fulfill the charge issued by the states to create the *next generation* of K-12 standards in order to help ensure that all students are college and career ready in literacy no later than the end of high school."

Why are new standards needed? In brief, because too many students are leaving high school unprepared for the literacy demands of the community college, college, university, or workplace. Too many students cannot independently read, make sense of, or make discerning judgments about demanding and complex text (especially informational and literary nonfiction); too many students cannot write clearly to show their understanding and reasoning, and use evidence and information to do so; too many students cannot listen thoughtfully and carefully; and too many students cannot express themselves clearly and cogently.

The Common Core State Standards in English Language Arts and Literacy are designed to address these problems. They point out clearly and forcefully that, in order to be competent and capable adults, our students must be able to think critically, read analytically and write clearly. The Standards lay out a carefully described framework for what it will take at each grade level in terms of literacy instruction so that, by the end of high school, virtually all students are well-prepared for education beyond high school, be it college, the workplace, or the military.

It is beyond the scope of this preface to take an exhaustive look at the standards. What we can point out here is that the goal of the Common Core Standards and the goal of Writing for Understanding are nearly identical. Writing for Understanding provides a proven and practical approach for addressing the Common Core ELA Standards in every teacher's classroom—so that every student is deeply literate, and every student is prepared for the world he encounters.

What are the Common Core Standards trying to accomplish?

Broadly, the Standards themselves state,

"As a natural outgrowth of meeting the charge to define college and career readiness, the Standards also lay out a vision of what it means to be a literate person in the twenty-first century. Indeed, the skills and understandings students are expected to demonstrate have wide applicability outside the classroom or workplace. Students who meet the Standards readily undertake the close, attentive reading that is at the heart of understanding and enjoying complex works of literature.

They habitually perform the critical reading necessary to pick carefully through the staggering amount of information available today in print and digitally. They actively seek the wide, deep, and thoughtful engagement with high-quality literary and informational texts that builds knowledge, enlarges experience, and broadens worldviews. They reflexively demonstrate the cogent reasoning and use of evidence that is essential to both private deliberation and responsible citizenship in a democratic republic" (p. 3).

These Common Core Standards, lofty as their goal may seem, are premised on the understanding that at the heart of these goals is the ability of students to read and write well and thoughtfully, to listen carefully and discerningly, to speak clearly, and to think critically. If we as educators do not make these priorities, we cannot hope to reach all our students—the strugglers as well as the quick learners, the children from poverty as well as the children of advantage.

It is, after all, a matter of equity: what will happen to these individual students if we fail them? It is also a matter of practicality: what will happen to our nation if so many of our students cannot meet the demands of college and the workplace?

What do the Common Core Standards emphasize?

Key aspects of the Standards include:

• **an emphasis on complex text for *all students***

Texts can be appropriately complex in many ways, including vocabulary, length and structure of sentences, and sophistication of ideas. Reading and making meaning from increasingly complex text, both literary and informational, is at the heart of the Common Core Standards. Rich and complex text itself reflects deep, often nuanced knowledge on the part of the writer – being able to do the hard work to grapple with it successfully on the part of the reader is a huge part of what it means to be a "literate person in the twenty-first century".

• an emphasis on integrated literacy

Reading, writing, speaking and listening cannot be separated and still be effectively taught. Writing is taught in the context of reading and discussing complex text; literacy instruction overall is shared by everyone within the school. With the depth of the Common Core Standards, and the emphasis on authentically complex text of all types, this integration cannot be lip service. It must be actual, it must be significant, and it must be sustained.

• an emphasis on building strong and deep content knowledge

Literacy is not fragmented; rather, it is the result of consistent, purposeful attention on the part of teachers and curriculum to building a strong and deep "base of knowledge over a wide range of subject matter". This is the opposite of the "today we're reading about dinosaurs, tomorrow about tomatoes" approach to text. Instead, it recognizes that students will learn to read well and deeply only if they are given the opportunity to build strong and deep domains of knowledge and understanding that matter.

• an emphasis on expository, text-based writing

The Standards do include narrative writing in some form at all grade levels. However, the majority of the writing standards are expository: arguments (what some have called persuasive writing), and informative / explanatory, especially by middle and high school but even at younger grades. This is writing that is consistently evidence-based, with evidence coming from working with rich text and other rich materials in various ways, and thinking about it honestly and critically. It is also writing that demonstrates deep understanding of and clear thinking about its subject.

So, what's the connection to *Writing for Understanding*?

Writing for Understanding is premised on the understanding that writing well is ultimately about making meaning thoughtfully, and communicating that meaning clearly. When a piece of writing is effective, at any grade level, it is a *coherent chunk of meaning* to both the writer and the reader.

Writing for Understanding recognizes that no student (nor anyone else, for that matter) can write effectively if she does not have solid knowledge and understanding about her subject, and does not have a clear structure through which to think about, construct, and communicate that knowledge.

With this in mind, it becomes essential in *Writing for Understanding* for teachers to plan intentionally—to have a clear idea of what level and type of understanding they want students to be able to show in writing, and then to plan for both content understanding, writing knowledge, and structure so that all students—*all students*—are able to write effectively.

Very often, building this knowledge and understanding requires helping students make meaning from rich text. When it does, reading that text cannot be watered down, and it cannot be left to chance. Teachers must help students work with the text purposefully, thoughtfully, thoroughly, even painstakingly - *exactly the sort of reading that the Common Core Standards describe.*

Essentially, building this knowledge and understanding requires deep, rich domain knowledge. One cannot write effectively about something which is minimally, or superficially, or only partially understood. When Writing for Understanding teachers plan for effective writing, they are considering a domain of knowledge about which students need to know.

The size of this domain can and does vary. But what is clear is that when teachers plan so that *all students* can write effectively, they are in effect articulating the domain that students will come to know well, and helping the students synthesize that genuine understanding in clear writing. Again, this is *exactly the sort of writing that the Common Core Standards describe.*

In this book, we describe an integrated approach to teaching writing that emphasizes close reading and critical thinking while at the same time teaching specific skills that will help students become clear and effective writers. Overall, Writing for Understanding recognizes the power of writing as a tool for making meaning. Like the Common Core, we believe that when teachers plan thoughtfully and intentionally so that this power is in the hands of all students, we all – the student herself, and all the rest of us—benefit.

A Message to Teachers

It was a December afternoon, and the twenty-seven third- and fourth-grade students who filled the classroom during the day had long since boarded the school buses and gone home for the evening. Their young teacher should have been going home, too— she had supper to fix, papers to correct, phone calls to make for her family, laundry to do.

Home, however, did not appear to be in sight; there was still so much to do here. She contemplated the classroom, large yellow crate in hand. Everywhere she looked, the evidence of her students' ongoing hard work was evident. For the past week, they had all been engulfed in writing dinosaur reports. The dedicated young teacher had taken this responsibility very seriously. Students were working in pairs, and each pair had selected for research the dinosaur that interested its members the most. Each pair had its own large plastic envelope, in which students were keeping their materials: books on the dinosaur in question, pictures, clay for making a dinosaur model. Further, each crate contained a clipboard, with a planning web for the students to use to decide what their dinosaur report should include. Each group even had a number and a place to put the number. As they needed her help with anything, the teacher had thought, the students would put up their number, then wait for her to get to them for help (meanwhile busily and productively occupying themselves).

In short, the teacher had planned well. These third and fourth graders were well equipped for reading and thinking and writing about their dinosaur of choice!

But somehow, things had not worked out.

Standing there with the empty crate, the young teacher mulled over the past few days. The students needed help, lots of it, with reading their dinosaur materials, and very few of them could figure out which material they actually needed. The planning web's purpose was elusive; many students didn't know what to put in it. The teacher could see that many, maybe most of her third and fourth graders, needed her help with navigating the material, then figuring out what to put on the web. She could see, when she had a chance to look up as she raced around the room from group to group, that even the strong students were copying down anything and everything about their dinosaur, whether they understood it or not. Others, while waiting for their teacher to get to them, had gone off task and were playing with the clay—noisily.

Suddenly, the young teacher found her eyes filling with tears. What had she been thinking? How could she possibly help so many people? And if she didn't help them, what would these twenty-seven curious, eager, but not-yet-very-skilled third and fourth graders take away from this dinosaur report-writing experience?

It is our guess that there is not a writing teacher in the country who has not experienced some version of this scenario. Incredibly dedicated, hardworking teachers everywhere have tried valiantly to help students write—not just reports, but responses to text, stories, reflections, poetry, persuasive position papers. With many students needing help (of course! writing is a challenging task!), these teachers have found themselves unable to meet the needs they can see in their students. Trying to work with one or two students at a time, nearly always with different material, they struggle to help all of their students read the material, understand it, decide what to use, then figure out how to write something that makes sense. The barriers—for the student struggling to read and organize ideas, for the teacher struggling to reach each one—are enormous.

In a genuinely academically diverse classroom—as most public school classrooms are—trying to effectively provide writing instruction has been a Herculean task. Often, working with writing this way, teachers have found themselves making impossible choices: either find a way to work adequately with each child or group in what amounts to tutorials (at lunch, at 7:00 in the morning, during recess, after school, for weeks), or else settle for some number of students producing substandard writing—writing which makes sense to neither the writer nor a reader.

We are writing this book for those teachers, to let them know that there is an alternative. The book describes an approach to teaching we have called *Writing for Understanding*. Its premise is that writing is about constructing and communicating meaning. The product itself—the student's written work—shows that the writer knows and understands what he is talking about and can communicate it clearly to readers. In order to write effectively to show meaning, students—at any grade level, no matter what they are writing about—need to have four elements in place. They need:

- knowledge, and solid understanding of that knowledge

- a focus through which to think about and work with that knowledge and understanding

- a structure to develop their knowledge and understanding

- grade-level control over writing conventions

Writing for Understanding is for teachers. The book lays out a manageable, effective approach to teacher planning so that students have access to all of those elements, especially the first three, before they sit down to write. Based on the principle of "backward design" (Wiggins and McTighe), it conceptualizes planning for writing instruction in terms of key elements. These are:

Central Ideas

What is it that I want students to understand about this *content?* What understandings about the craft of writing do I want them to grasp?

Focusing Question

What question will I pose so that students can see how to approach this thinking/writing in a specific, appropriate, manageable way?

Building and Processing Working Knowledge

How am I going to make sure that students know enough about this subject by the end to actually be able to write about it?

Structure

How will my students know how to construct/build this piece of writing so that their thinking is clear, both to them as writers and to the readers of their work?

Writing

How will my students draft/revise so that their final writing is clearly focused, organized, and developed to show understanding of the central ideas?

In the book, we will explain each of these elements in detail, making ample use of student work and teacher think-alouds as we go. In the Introduction, we lay out the argument for paying close attention to the role of understanding in the composition process. Chapter One takes a close look at what we mean by "effective writing" and explains the *Writing for Understanding* approach to planning and instruction in greater detail. In Chapter Two, we begin examining each planning element listed above, working with the idea of planning for a focus for student thinking and writing. Chapter Three explains the importance of planning for the acquisition of knowledge and understanding in both content and writing craft, and offers examples of what this can look like. In Chapter Four, we examine the role of structure in writing and show some ways in which teachers can plan for structure in writing. Chapter Five works with drafting and embedded revision (formative assessment on the part of both student and teacher), while Chapter Six examines the question of transfer, moving away from guided instruction to more independent work. And transfer is the ultimate goal of *Writing for Understanding:* the point where students have internalized the ability to write effectively and can apply it in new situations.

In a *Writing for Understanding* classroom, what might the dinosaur reports experience described at the beginning look like? It could take many different forms (*Writing for Understanding* is *not* a lockstep, rigid approach), but here is one possibility:

Twenty-seven third and fourth graders are sitting in small groups. Each group has chosen a dinosaur to research together, and the students are excited about that (what's not to love about dinosaurs?).

First, though, they are going to write, together, about Ankylosaurus, the dinosaur that they have researched together as a whole class. On the wall is a large, colorful web full of highly organized group notes and pictures contributed by the class, their guided, shared work over the past week. Their focus for the notes, "Ankylosaurus was a creature that was well adapted to its environment," has determined how those notes have been structured—every note reminds the students just how well adapted Ankylosaurus was, in many specific ways.

The teacher pulls out the overhead projector. "Here we go, everybody!" she says. "We now know so much about this truly amazing Ankylosaurus that we're ready to write. Today, we'll begin with an introduction—we need to let the reader know a bit of background about dinosaurs in general before we launch into our own focus—'Ankylosaurus was a creature well adapted to its environment.' So, scientists, what do you think our reader might need to know about dinosaurs in this introduction?"

Together, the class composes an introduction for the group piece. By the time students have completed this process, they will have a model—a good idea of what their own piece will look like, what a focused, organized, well-written, well-understood "well-adapted dinosaur" paper can be. When they come to start reading and discussing their own dinosaur paper, they will bring to that process a strong sense of this final product and the understanding embodied by it.

And the young teacher in this *Writing for Understanding* classroom? She knows that every one of her students is engaged in a task that makes sense to him. She knows that every one of her students is working with knowledge he understands. She knows that she will get a range of achievement, but that her third and fourth graders will *all* be able to construct and communicate meaning in these dinosaur reports.

For students to have genuine access to instruction like this, teachers need help planning, so that students can write successfully and effectively and even joyfully, and still have time for recess

—and so that the teacher still has time to do her laundry. This book is written to help make that teacher planning possible, manageable, and workable.

—Eloise Ginty
Joey Hawkins
Karen LeClaire Kurzman
Diana Leddy
Jane Miller

Section I

Writing Matters:
What the Research Says,
What Experience Tells Us

Introduction: Fresh Ink

"Some pig!"

It had been a memorable summer on the Zuckerman farm. Wilbur the pig had spent his day eating the best slops the farm had to offer. The goslings had hatched. Best of all, Charlotte the gray barn spider had made friends with him and filled his days with friendship and happiness. Charlotte and Wilbur had gotten to know each other well. Each knew what the other liked to eat, how the other thought, and what the other cared about.

So when Wilbur learned that Mr. Zuckerman planned to turn him into bacon, Charlotte went into action. It was imperative that Mr. Zuckerman understand what she knew to be the truth about Wilbur. (In fact, she needed to *persuade* Mr. Zuckerman of her point of view—Charlotte was nothing if not aware of her audience!)

She thought and thought, and she came up with a plan.

She wrote. Choosing her words with great care, using all the technical skill she could muster, Charlotte turned her web into a thing of meaning—a clear and powerful expression of the essential truth about her friend Wilbur.

"Some pig!"

Charlotte, the gray barn spider in E.B. White's immortal classic *Charlotte's Web,* was not writing because she needed to pick an interesting topic and she had to come up with something to say. She did not write a first draft to show she knew how to use a process.

Nor was Charlotte writing from a sketchy knowledge base. She had not spent ten minutes hastily researching facts about pigs. She had spent the summer with Wilbur; she knew him well. From that deep understanding had grown a very personal connection. Wilbur was Charlotte's friend. Charlotte's writing saved his life.

Writing is not always about life and death, but in the end, writing is always about meaning. From the efficiently constructed grocery list, to the first grader's tribute to his mother on Mother's Day, to the fourth-grade essay on how chickadees survive in the winter, to the eulogy composed for a dear friend, to the investigation of the effects of global warming on polar bears, a piece of writing has meaning for the writer—and for the reader. Such writing can only come from knowledge and understanding.

Writing Matters

"Writing is how students connect the dots in their knowledge" (National Commission on Writing 2003).

In 2003, the National Commission on Writing issued its alarm about the state of writing instruction in American schools. Calling its report "The Neglected 'R': The Need For a Writing Revolution," the commission challenged American public education, primary through university, to teach all students to write effectively, clearly, and thoughtfully.

Why does writing matter so much?

At its most basic level, writing is how we keep track of the thoughts that are important to us. Ancient Egypt became one of the first "civilizations" based partly on its people's ability to write. The culture's system of hieroglyphics was used primarily for record keeping. Who owed what to whom? Where was that grain stored, and how much was there? Knowing how to manipulate the characters was so important that only a few people, the scribes, were trained how to do so and, as the keepers of written language, they held the reins of substantial power and influence in their society.

Over the centuries the importance of writing has remained constant. In the Middle Ages, monks spent years holed up in monasteries across Europe, laboriously copying ancient Greek and Roman texts so that the knowledge of the world they contained would not be forgotten. William Tyndale translated the Christian Bible into English so that ordinary people, not just the priesthood, would be able to read it, and was burned at the stake for his efforts. Thomas Jefferson labored over the Declaration of Independence with his quill pen and ink and changed the world. Slaves in the cotton fields of the American South created spirituals and stories of hope which they sang over and over, and eventually wrote down so that others could sing those words about those hopes as well.

As human beings, we have a great and fundamental urge to make meaning from our experience, from the most basic and mundane to the most profound levels. Language is not the only tool for this, but it is one of the most powerful. And written language is the way we both construct that meaning, capture it, hone it, and communicate it.

Writing for All

Writing remains a powerful synthesizing tool. In an era when people are deluged with information and ideas, the ability to make sense of them and to express that understanding in coherent writing is a critical skill.

It is true that most of us do not spend our lives with a yellow legal pad in hand. What is also true, however, is that we are frequently faced with tasks that require us to think critically in writing—because clear, effective writing is really a reflection of clear thinking. When we are faced with making a recommendation between two competing insurance plans, we need to be able to summarize their key points and explain clearly which is better—a writing task that reflects and communicates clear thinking. When we are applying for a job, we need to be able to articulate compellingly why we are a well-suited candidate for that job—again, a writing task that requires and reflects clear thinking. When we write to a car dealer requesting help on a recall notice, we need to be able to formulate the problem clearly—once again, obviously, a thinking/writing task.

These are not tasks reserved for academics or people in high places of influence. These are tasks that ordinary people face on a regular basis. To the degree that we can use writing to manage those tasks, we are able to connect with and navigate the challenging world in which we all live. To the degree that we cannot use writing to synthesize, understand, and communicate, we operate from a position of disadvantage, even powerlessness.

Writing is not easy. Because it is not passive but active, not receptive but generative, it often involves hard mental work. This is precisely what makes it a powerful tool to put into the hands of students.

Writing and Equity

One of the most ardent proponents of writing, particularly nonfiction or expository writing, is Doug Reeves (2000). In his work he describes the "90/90/90 schools" as successful schools where 90% of the students are on free or reduced lunch, 90% are members of minorities, and 90% are achieving high academic standards. According to Reeves, one of the key common factors in all of these schools is frequent opportunity for students to use nonfiction writing. Reeves writes,

The benefits of such an emphasis on writing appear to be twofold. First, students process information in a much clearer way when they are required to write an answer. They "write to think" and, thus, gain the opportunity to clarify their own thought processes. Second, teachers have the opportunity to gain rich and complex diagnostic information about why students respond to an academic challenge the way they do.... The association between writing and performance in other academic disciplines was striking, and gets to the heart of the curriculum choices that teachers must make. (Reeves 2000, pp. 189–190).

Reeves's work pulls no punches. If we are serious about raising the achievement of our most disadvantaged students, about making sure they are in the game, then writing in school—frequently, clearly, tied to understanding —matters.

The work of Ruby Payne, a frequent contributor to the national discussion about equity for disadvantaged students, supports this point as well. She points out that one of the greatest disadvantages students from poverty face is their lack of flexibility of language. The world of reading, writing, work, and school all require the use of what Payne calls "formal register" language, including the use of complete sentences and the precise choice of words. On the other hand, "casual register" language, the only language to which disadvantaged students typically have access, is much less flexible, "characterized by a 400–500 word vocabulary, broken sentences, and many non-verbal assists" (Payne 1996). To her, direct instruction in language use in school is essential, including direct instruction that makes full use of writing.

If we are serious about equity, then, we need to be serious about helping all students become effective writers.

Writing and Work

Writing also matters on the job. For some years the private sector of business has been sounding the alarm about the writing skills of the workforce. National organizations such as Achieve, the Education Trust, the American Diploma Project, and the recent ACT report have all extensively documented the lack of overall preparation for the workforce and for higher education, as well as the billions that are spent in remediation. The National Commission on Writing, too, has continued to call for much greater attention to writing instruction in schools, to prepare students first to get a job and then be able to perform its duties. Its most recent report highlights the need for solid writing skills in state government work. Its survey found that states spend $221 million dollars annually upgrading the writing skills of their employees. According to Bob Kerrey, president of New School University in New York, former senator and governor from Nebraska, and chair of the commission,

> Clear communication is an essential government function in a democratic society.... Because writing is how agencies communicate with each other and their constituents, all of us have a stake in the clarity and accuracy of government writing" (National Commission on Writing 2005).

Challenge of Teaching Students to Write

Teaching students to write effectively has been consistently challenging. The National Writing Project, which has contributed enormously and consistently to the effort to help teachers help students learn to write, has recently produced *Because Writing Matters*. This book chronicles the inception of the "writing process" movement in the early 1970's, when such researchers as Donald Graves and Janet Emig began studying the ways writers go about the task of thinking and producing polished writing (NWP, 2006).

Their work evolved into what has become known to teachers as the writing process, an approach that has stressed the importance of stages in writing: prewriting, drafting, revising, editing, publishing. Over the past thirty-plus years, many teachers and schools have instituted various incarnations of process writing, often in the form of writing workshops made popular by such researchers as Lucy Calkins and Nancie Atwell. In some states, like Vermont, writing portfolios based on the writing process have been supported in schools by state departments of education in various ways.

Indeed, there is evidence that in classrooms where attention has actually been paid to some elements of the writing process, there has been some increase in student achievement in writing. In the 2002 National Assessment of Educational Progress (NAEP), there were some small overall gains in student achievement nationwide (NAEP 2003). More significantly, a few years earlier, in the 1998 NAEP assessment of writing, the report found that students who planned their writing, discussed their writing frequently with a teacher, and kept writing portfolios were more successful than students who did not (NWP 2006, p. 44).

However, more than thirty years since the writing process began to enter classrooms, writing is still a challenge for students, and teachers struggle to find the best ways to help them. The majority of eighth-grade students, even in NAEP's highest performing states of Connecticut, Massachusetts, and Vermont, have not yet reached the proficient level, and in most states the level of proficiency in writing is low to very low (NAEP 2003).

The need for help for teachers is clear: the writing process, as we have understood it, is not enough.

Some Clues: What Works?

Charlotte was onto something. She knew Wilbur well before she set to work on writing in her web, and she worked hard on her web missives. From Charlotte, we learn that writing depends on knowledge, it requires careful attention to structure, and it takes time.

Interestingly, NAEP agrees. In 1998 it asked the Educational Testing Service (ETS) and the National Writing Project to study a sample of classrooms where more than two thirds of the students had strong achievement on the fourth- and eighth-grade NAEP. NAEP wanted to know what kinds of classroom assignments produced strong writers. They found that some degree of personal choice in writing matters, as does audience—both staples of "process writing."

But they also found that other things matter, including:

- *Thinking.* Students needed to be given the opportunity to reflect on their knowledge, to analyze information, to synthesize. They need questions and assignments that ask them to "transform the information from the reading material in order to complete the writing assignment" (NWP 2006)—in other words, to construct real meaning.

- *A framework for organizing and developing ideas.* Students do not just figure out how to organize their ideas. They need assignments that show them the way—if not literally map it, then at least point in a familiar direction.

- *Frequent opportunity to write.* A 2002 report on National Writing Project classrooms in five states added another significant factor that matters: time. It found that "NWP teachers spend far more time on writing instruction than most fourth-grade teachers across the country. Eighty-three percent of NWP classroom teachers in a study conducted by the Academy for Educational Development spent more than ninety minutes per week on writing activities, compared with just 31 percent of fourth-grade teachers nationally" (NWP 2006, p. 49).

This does *not* mean that all National Writing Project classrooms produce more effective writers (*Writing Next,* 2007, p. 20). It does, however, indicate a correlation between how much students write and how well and thoughtfully they write.

The Question: So, what else is needed?

It would seem from these reports that, as a profession, teachers indeed already know all we need to know about what works in writing instruction, and all that is needed is more professional development around writing process and the will to use it.

In our work around Vermont, however, we have found that, as valuable as the writing process is, it is not enough. It has been significant, necessary, and vital, but it has left out some key pieces. The ETS report to NAEP emphasized the value of a thoughtful question to drive student writing, with the clear message that writing is about thinking. We find, however, that the "thoughtful question" is not enough to produce effective writing. Our work has convinced us that, even with a thoughtful question, many students fail when they write. This failure occurs not because they do not use the writing process with a thoughtful question, *but because they don't have sufficient knowledge in the first place.* No matter how thought-provoking the question is, one cannot reflect on knowledge one does not have. One cannot analyze information that is sketchy, inaccurate, or poorly understood. One cannot synthesize from nothing. It is up to teachers, then, to provide activities and experiences that give students knowledge and help them construct meaning from that knowledge.

The report also referred to the importance of scaffolding for students. The implication is that students need a clear and specific sense of direction when they write, to help them understand how to put the piece of writing together. We find, however, that the minimal level of scaffolding recommended in the ETS report is not sufficient when students are actively learning to write. A student cannot invent a structure she has never seen before. She cannot intuit the concept of "thesis statement" if she has never worked to develop one. For the most part, she cannot inductively figure out how to support an idea with textual evidence. If she has never seen or worked with thoughtful conclusions, she does not know how they work or how to construct one. If she has not read or written "on the other hand" when contrasting ideas, she does not have access to that structural language as a tool.

In fact, our work in Vermont has shown us that structures are more than tools for organizing ideas. Forms and structures in writing are not merely techniques to be learned, they are techniques *for* learning. The act and process of selecting, ordering, and developing ideas while writing pushes students to find meaning, to construct understanding. We have found that when we introduce students, from primary grades through high school, to a variety of flexible structures and give them guided practice in using them, they become able to "own" those structures in their own thinking. Those structures become a vehicle for thinking. Students are able to use them to make meaning in their own minds and on paper, meaning that is clear to both the writer and the reader.

In short, we have found in our work with our students at all grade levels—both low-achieving and high-achieving—that in order to write effectively about anything, students need depth of knowledge in the topic about which they will be writing. They also need a clear understanding of what they want to say about that knowledge, as well as a sense of how to build the particular piece of writing they will build.

The Answer: *Writing for Understanding*

Over many years of work with students of all ages and abilities in many different classrooms, we have developed an approach to writing that builds our findings into the writing process. We call this approach *Writing for Understanding.*

Based on the idea that writing is ultimately about meaning, it places a premium on understanding. Students need to understand the ideas with which they are working. They also need to understand the structures and writing elements they are using. And they need all of this not just for this particular writing task. They also need it for transfer, so that they can apply it to other thinking/writing tasks down the road.

To that end, we have developed and tested an approach to instruction that is practical, manageable, and useful. It has three premises:

- *Backward design.*   We are indebted to the *Understanding by Design* work of Grant Wiggins and Jay McTighe. We base our approach on the idea that teachers plan best when they "plan backward" for instruction, starting by identifying the understandings they want students to communicate in writing by the end of the unit, then planning backward for specific instruction, in *both content knowledge and writing structures,* so that all students are able to produce a solid, thoughtful piece of writing at the end.

- *An emphasis on understanding.*   In order to write effectively, students require two types of understanding. First, we have seen students struggle with writing for many reasons, but one of the most frequent and least addressed is knowledge and understanding of content: too often, students do not know what they are talking about. An essential part of backward design planning, then, involves planning for students to develop deep content knowledge.

It also includes understanding of writing craft. Our work is geared towards students' being able to write, not just about the ideas in a particular piece, but as a transferrable skill. It is geared toward students' gaining conceptual and structural knowledge of elements of writing, standards, and genres of writing—expressive and informational/expository. We want students to internalize and increasingly "own" the concept of introduction, of transitions, of images, of all of those elements it takes to write well, so that they can later transfer them to new writing situations.

- *Direct instruction.*   We have all seen students benefit from direct instruction (and then lots of guided practice) in many ways: riding a bike, making a foul shot, parallel parking, being polite to siblings. Our approach incorporates direct instruction, as needed, into every aspect of an instructional unit, so that by the end students have a piece of writing that is clearly structured, well developed, and thoughtful—and a set of skills that are on their way to being transferrable.

This direct instruction includes frequent, built-in oral processing. It is true that sophisticated writers can sometimes write more effectively than they can speak. For student writers, however, we find that this is rarely true. *Students cannot write what they cannot speak.* This is as true for high school students as it is for first graders.

Oral processing before writing and during writing, then, is a fundamental aspect of our Writing for Understanding *approach.* It allows students to "work out" their ideas in guided conversation before they have to work with them in writing.

Does *Writing for Understanding* Work?

How well does this approach to content writing work in a heterogeneous classroom? First, it's important to recognize that *Writing for Understanding* is not a magic bullet. It does not guarantee that every student in a class will achieve the same high standards in writing. It does not mean that the student writing never shows misunderstanding or that all students show equal insight or depth of comprehension of what they are writing about.

What we have found, however, is that "this approach to writing keeps all students firmly in the game" (Hawkins, 2006). In a classroom community of thinking, speaking, and writing, it allows students to flourish where they may well not have flourished—or even really engaged. *Writing for Understanding* allows both high-achieving and struggling students to work with written language in a way that, for those students, produces real meaning about real content.

Assessment results bear this out. In the Vermont classrooms where we work, state level test scores and other assessments in writing have consistently shown a great majority of the students (often including special education students) achieving high standards in writing. Other schools that have consistently used a *Writing for Understanding* approach have seen similar impressive results at the classroom and school level. A recent unpublished action-research study conducted by Vermont Institutes bears this out. In 2003/2004, Vermont Institutes, a not-for-profit support program in Vermont, trained fourth- and eighth-grade teachers in fourteen classrooms in different schools in *Writing for Understanding*. Of the fourteen classrooms, nearly all of whose schools had a substantial number of free and reduced lunch students, all but one showed substantial improvement on the writing assessment between 2003 and 2004.

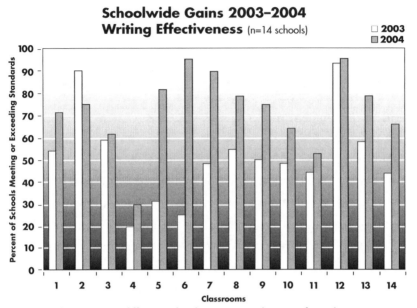

Schoolwide Gains 2003–2004
Writing Effectiveness (n=14 schools)

□ 2003
▨ 2004

Fourteen classrooms in different schools participated in an informal action-research study of the effectiveness of *Writing for Understanding* instruction

What has really driven us to write this book, however, is the reaction of teachers "in the trenches." One middle school teacher wrote, "More students have positive feelings this year than any other year I've taught. This, I believe, is a result of the confidence they've gained as a result of their successful writing experiences in school. Now, nearly all of my students can write focused, organized essays."

A fourth-grade teacher wrote about the value of taking the time for students to process information before writing: "working through the charts was great and really worthwhile! It was helpful to *all* students, creating independence [for them]. It made me think about activities and whether or not they really pertained to the working knowledge." Another fourth-grade teacher described making sure her special education students did not leave the classroom during writing time, as they were benefiting so much from the direct instruction. A second-grade teacher wrote that "children are much more excited about writing! Since a lot is done now to teach children writing through visual, auditory and kinesthetic means, thus addressing various learning styles, more children are able to be involved in the instruction and practice of writing. Children have increased abilities to create, support and reflect on a focus in their writing."

As teachers ourselves, we are acutely aware that, for students, a great deal rides on what happens in the classroom. Teachers matter, and how they teach matters. We hope that our book will be of help to them.

Chapter One:

What is *Writing for Understanding*?

How do we know when a piece of student writing is effective and when it is not? Do we all agree on what effective student writing is?

In our experience, the good news is that while there is certainly room for variety (in fact, great variety) in writing, and emphasis varies on what matters most, there is general consensus about the basic elements that constitute effective writing. In this chapter we will describe those "elements of effective writing" and their relationship to understanding, then look more closely at the *Writing for Understanding* approach.

To do that, it's helpful to look at some student writing. What does ineffective writing look like? How is effective writing different?

Upper Elementary Informational Writing

A fifth-grade student wrote the following report about the Vietnam War and put it into her end-of-year writing portfolio. We don't know where the student got the information for the report;

it may have been from independent reading and research, it may have been from an interview, or it may have been from classroom content.

When the reader first looks at the piece, it looks like it may be an effective piece of writing. The spelling and punctuation seem to be in place, and the writer has used paragraphs in what seems to be an intentional way.

The Longest WAR!!!!!

The longest war was also known as the Vietnam War. Was it a good idea for the U.S.A. to help Southern Vietnam to keep their freedom? Yes, because we fight for freedom not letting people take over people. Two main topics involving this war are freedom and the fact that it was the longest war.

The reason I picked freedom is because I believe in freedom and they should have their own rights, own laws and be two different countries. They did succeed in this task as there is a North Vietnam and a South Vietnam today.

The Vietnam War was the longest war known to history. It started in 1957 and ended in 1975. It ended over two decades ago. There was a lot of blood shed and lives lost in this very long war. Because of the length of this war it is one that is still very much thought of in the minds of many adult Americans. The North and the South fought against each other and we helped South Vietnam.

What I learned about this war, which to me can for any war, is that war can mean you may or may

> not have a winner, but no matter what we always help and support the troops. I think war is scary and I don't really like the fact that people just can't be nice and treat one another as everyone should be treated.

However, after reading the piece, the reader is confused. The young writer has clearly invested time and energy in the writing. Her proofreading has been careful, and her engagement and interest in the idea of war seem unmistakable.

Yet the piece shows fragmented understanding in some places, actual misunderstanding in others. In fact, there are not two Vietnams today, so the U.S. did not "succeed in this task" as the young writer asserts. Further, the Vietnam War was not the "longest war known to history." What does the writer know about the Vietnam War that she is trying to tell us? What point is she trying to make about the war? In this piece, the writer herself seems to be confused. As a piece of writing, it cannot be called effective.

Primary Response to Text

A second-grade class in an urban school was working with response-to-text writing, a genre that helps students construct and communicate understanding of a literary or informational text. In this case, the class had read the *Catwings* series by Ursula Leguin. Below is one student's response to that reading experience.

> We read Catwings series by Ursula Leguin. the books are abut cats with wings and there many adventures and troubles they face. two of the mane characters, Jane and alexander are the same and different in many ways.

Jane and alxander are the same in many ways. thay both ran awy from home to see New things. they both had fears to over come, Jane was so terrified of rats Jane coul only hiss HATE! t scwed me! axander was so afraid of hights that he coul not get doun by himself.

Jane and alexander are also different in many ways. first of all Jane has older siblings and alexander has younger siblings. Second Jane is so tarafide of rats she coud not tock on the other hand alexander is afrade of bul dogs. therd of all Jane was born in ally (a stray cat). and alexander was born in a house. (**not** ally cat).

As you can see Jane and allexander are the same and different in many ways. becous the more diffrenses you have with somewon the more simaleriteas youl find with them. thow your thinking is all your own your feelings can be the same. Even your werst enemy has many simalaratys.

This second grader does not yet have complete, consistent control of capitalization and spelling. However, the writer knows what he is talking about. He has a clear sense of the direction his thoughts are heading, expressed in his controlling idea ("Jane and alexander are the same and different in many ways"). He uses the structure of the piece to develop his ideas, switching paragraphs when his ideas need to shift. The writer knows the book he is writing about. He is able to go back to the text to retrieve specific ideas to develop his focus statement. At the end, the writer reflects on some big ideas, connecting his understanding of the book to his own observations about life. As a piece of writing, this one is effective.

Middle-school Persuasive Writing

The eighth-grade student who wrote this persuasive piece was in an integrated history and language arts class. He had participated in a unit on World War I, including a simulation of a debate that occurred in 1919, in which the United States Senate was trying to decide whether to ratify the Treaty of Versailles and join the newly formed League of Nations. This is the final draft of a speech in which the student, as "senator," was trying to persuade his constituents that he had made the correct decision in voting that the U.S. join the League.

Great people of North Dakota,

I, Senator McCumber, have just participated in a debate regarding whether or not America should sign the Treaty of Versailles, and in doing so, join the League of Nations. The League of Nations is a unified group of nations dedicated to the preservation of peace. The League is designed to deal with international issues, adjudicating differences between countries instead of them going directly to combat.

Now, in the interests of the great state of North Dakota, I voted in favor of the treaty with no reservations. We need a fair treaty to prevent future wars as horrible as the Great War was. After the war, the central powers composed the Treaty of Versailles to create the League of Nations in an attempt to ward off future conflicts. We cannot have another war as horrible as this one. I believe, because of that, that we need a fair treaty, equal to all its members, that will restrict the use of new weapons, and prevent future wars from breaking out.

First, the Treaty and the League will control the use of new weapons. As stated in Article VII, "One of its (the League's) jobs will be to come up with a plan for reducing the number of weapons around the world (arms reduction)." This means that the League will be in charge of weapons issues. This will cause heavily armed countries to demilitarize and make it less possible for war to break out. This is good because heavily armed countries generally end up using those arms in some way.

Another reason why I believe we need to sign the Treaty with no reservations is we need a treaty that is fair to all its members. Reservations (proposed by the League's opponents) would give America too much power within the league, thus allowing America to bend the rules of the League to suit its own will. This would cause unrest in the League, possibly causing America to make enemies. This could lead to another war. The treaty should be as fair as possible.

Yet another reason why I voted for America to sign the treaty is the fact it would prevent future wars from breaking out. The way the League is designed, it would give plenty of time for the League to settle the countries' differences with a fair and equal compromise. If war were to break out, the council members in the League would all help in defending each other, thus ending the war as quickly as possible with as few deaths as possible. The treaty would prevent war from happening or end the fighting as quickly as possible.

Some people say that we shouldn't join the League because we would be intervening in foreign affairs, that it would cause another war. How can you not intervene when 8 million people died in the last war? How can you stand there with a clear conscience when you know you could have prevented all that carnage from ever happening? The League will help countries settle their differences with plenty of time to talk it over. Six months for the countries to listen to the council's advice, and after that another three months before they can mobilize. If we join the League, we will keep anything like the Great War from happening again.

In conclusion, the Treaty of Versailles needs to be signed so the League will be put into affect. The League of Nations will prevent war from breaking out, restrict weapons development and militarism, and keep us from the horrors of another Great War.

Thank you.

After reading this piece, the reader has learned something about the League of Nations and some of the arguments both for and against the United States' joining it. The writer takes a clear position, organizes his argument well, and supports his ideas persuasively with real, specific information and ideas (the provisions the League would make for nations to discuss their differences, the urgent need to prevent millions more deaths as happened in the Great War). He knows that use of a counter-argument to bolster one's own position is an important aspect of the critical thinking involved in persuasive writing, and he has done so, skillfully ("Some people say that we shouldn't join the League because we would be intervening in foreign affairs"...). Because of the writer's intentional, informed use of ideas within a clear persuasive structure, the reader comes away with a deeper understanding of the issue than he had before reading. Like the writer of "The Longest War," this student is engaged with, even passionate about, his ideas. Unlike "The Longest War," this piece is clear and informative. As a piece of writing, it is effective.

The Elements of Effective Writing

These pieces of student writing help shed light on the common elements of effective writing, no matter what grade level and genre. What are those common elements?

What NAEP Tells Us

NAEP (The National Assessment of Education Progress) tests students in writing at regular intervals. NAEP is the yardstick against which state writing standards in on-demand writing are measured, so the way NAEP defines proficient writing is important.

In its 2003 report to the nation, NAEP defined fourth graders as "proficient" in on-demand writing when they are "able to produce an organized response…that shows an understanding of the writing task they have been assigned. Their writing should include details that support and develop their main idea, and it should show that these students are aware of the audience they are expected to address" (NAEP 2003, p. 9).

In eighth grade, proficiency builds from the fourth grade description. NAEP wrote that students "should be able to produce a detailed and organized response…that shows an understanding of both the writing task they have been assigned and the audience they are expected to address. Their writing should include precise language and varied sentence structure, and it may show analytical, evaluative, or creative thinking."

Twelfth-grade writing at the "proficient" level moves on from there. According to NAEP, students who are proficient in on-demand writing "should be able to produce an effectively organized and fully developed response...that uses analytical, evaluative, or creative thinking. Their writing should include details that support and develop the main idea of the piece, and it should show that these students are able to use precise language and variety in sentence structure to engage the audience they are expected to address."

In short, NAEP defines proficient writing at any grade level as having a controlling idea, an organizing structure, adequate elaboration, an awareness of audience, appropriate word choice and variety of sentence structure, and, as students mature in age, increasing sophistication of thought.

But NAEP actually implies more than this. In addition, by implication, the thinking communicated in the piece has to be clear and credible. Prompted writing on a national scale cannot depend on specific, common knowledge of content, but it can and does depend on a student's sense of reasonableness. By implication, then, clarity and reasonableness in thought are part of NAEP's definition of effective writing. *In other words, effective writing is inseparable from clear thinking.*

Others in the Field Agree

There is widespread agreement in the field among teachers of writing at any grade level about what essentially constitutes successful, effective writing. From the widely used "6 + 1 Traits" to state standards around the country, these elements of successful, effective writing are visible. Different approaches may use different terminology; they may and do group elements of effective writing differently on scoring rubrics. In the end, however, there is consensus on what effective writing is, what might be called the "grandmother of all writing standards." Effective writing includes:

- *Focus.* To be clear and effective, every piece of writing must have a single focus. This is true for a grocery list and a literary analysis, a letter to Aunt Martha and a PhD thesis. Donald Murray puts this idea elegantly and forcefully in his *The Craft of Revision.* He writes,

  > First of all, I must answer the question: "What is the one thing I must say?" For years—decades—I fought this, wanting to say two things or three or more. No matter what clever designs I created, what rhetorical tricks I employed, what new approaches I created, they all collapsed in confusion. In writing my column and my textbooks, my poems and my novels, my essays and my articles, I could only say one thing. Everything in the piece of writing had to lead to or away from that single message.
  >
  > Focus makes sure that one meaning is emphasized, and once that is established everything in the piece of writing must support and develop that meaning. (2004)

- *Structure.* Structures can and do vary widely, but if a piece of writing is to be clear and coherent to both writer and reader, it must have a structure, an organizational pattern that makes sense for the focus. Typically, elements of structure include such elements as introductions, transitions, conclusions, the way ideas are chunked, and overall text structure.

- *Development of details, elaboration.* A writer needs to develop and support a focus, regardless of the structure she is using. The development will vary depending on the genre, the particular focus, the audience, the grade level of the student, or any of a number of other factors. Sometimes "details" means, quite simply, enough (accurate) information;

sometimes it means reflection or explaining; sometimes it means the creation of images; sometimes it means examples; the list goes on. Regardless of those specifics, however, students need to use details in a way that is appropriate for the piece of writing.

- *Appropriate voice and tone.* Again, voice and tone vary with the purpose of the piece, the developmental level of the child, and other circumstances. As writers grow in sophistication, they pay more and more attention to the tone of a piece—should it sound formal? Informal? Silly? Moving? Outraged? A writer needs to know how to work with voice and tone effectively.

- *Conventions.* Simply put, the conventions of Standard English matter. Students need to know how to spell and how to correct spelling; they need to know how to work with punctuation, usage, grammatically correct sentences, and the rest of the elements of Standard English, as appropriate to their grade level. Any particular piece of writing needs to reflect this basic mastery of conventions.

What is unspoken in all of these elements, of course, is meaning —the very purpose of the writing itself. A focus exists to direct the *meaning* that the writer is constructing. The structure the writer uses exists to help make that *meaning* clear. Details and information, ideas and images, are all present in an effective piece of writing to make *meaning* more accessible. Voice and tone, even conventions, are not ends in themselves—they are there in the service of *meaning*, first for the writer and then for the reader.

When we look back at the three young writers at the beginning of the chapter, the necessity of these agreed-upon elements seems very clear. The fifth grader writing about the Vietnam War certainly has voice—she feels strongly about war, and it shows in her writing. She has a sense of structure, and she has reasonable control over conventions for her age. But without a clear central idea to guide her, and without accurate or adequate knowledge, she cannot show understanding or communicate any real meaning.

The second-grade *Catwings* reader and writer, as well as the eighth-grade 1919 senator are both in a better position. Each has constructed and communicated meaning: their pieces both show solid knowledge of their subject (and engagement with it), are built around a controlling idea, and make use of clear structures to develop their thinking and get it across to an audience.

Teaching Effective Writing: What's Been Missing?

With general overall agreement on what effective writing looks like, why has it been so difficult to get most of our students to be able to write effectively?

The fundamental answer to that question, the central argument we make in this book, is that we have not, as teachers, paid enough attention to that unarticulated purpose of all writing: *to construct and communicate meaning.* As a result, we have not adequately addressed the relationship among knowledge, focus, and structure to achieve clarity and genuine understanding, for both writer and reader.

The reasons for that lack of attention are multiple, complex, and historical, and a full discussion of them is beyond the scope of this book. However, in general, gleaned from our own years in the classroom and working with many other teachers, a few reasons seem to stand out.

- *We are uncertain about what it takes to teach students to be able to write effectively.* As former students ourselves, we can all remember a time when we were struggling with a concept in class—perhaps chemistry, perhaps calculus, perhaps the role of symbolism in *The Scarlet Letter*. We can remember the frustration of asking a teacher to explain something to us that the teacher himself clearly understood, but which he was at a loss to explain to us. For someone who intuitively understands trigonometric functions, or symbolism, it can be baffling to try to break that down or find an illuminating explanation for a student who cannot.

Writing has been a lot like that. As teachers, we somehow figured out how to write, even without being taught (at least, we learned it well enough to get through!). But knowing how to write and teaching someone else how to write are two different things. Most teachers have no models to go by when faced with that challenge of teaching students to write. We have done a lot of *assigning* of writing, but we have not done much *teaching* of writing.

- *We are wary about helping students too much.* Teachers frequently express concern and confusion about their role in student writing. Sometimes, teachers worry that if they help students, they are "writing for them." In other cases, teachers are actively resistant to what they think of as "intervention" in students' writing. They sometimes see this as intrusion into a student's personal life and ideas, or a judgment on students' culture. In this view, direct instruction can be a form of unethical authoritarianism.

- *We equate effective writing with control over conventions.* Many of us who are teachers today remember when writing really was all about spelling and a plethora of comma rules. We remember getting papers back with a vast number of red marks (always red!), indicating where a comma was needed, an infinitive had been split, or a participle dangled. With such an emphasis on conventions, there was often little attention given to what the writer was actually trying to say.

- *We equate effective writing with strong voice.* Writing is a tool for expression, often personal expression. Sometimes, that "personal voice" has been so highly valued that it mattered more than anything else—more than organization, more than clarity, more than thoughtfulness. As long as writing showed how the writer really felt about something, it was sometimes assumed to be effective writing.

- *We equate effective writing with use of the writing process.* The writing process was developed over the past thirty-plus years as a reflection of the reality of how "real writers" write. It has been profoundly useful, and influential, in guiding the way many schools, probably most schools, organize their writing programs.

  Sometimes, however, "using the writing process" has become a goal in itself. There has been such emphasis on the process that there has sometimes been insufficient emphasis on the product, other than the requirement that it reflect the student's voice.

- *We overlook the relationship between oral and written language.* It is true that many professional writers, or skilled writers in general, do not need to "talk" their ideas before writing. Indeed, skilled writers often point out that writing is, for them, often an act of self-discovery—that in the act of writing, they are able to synthesize their ideas in ways they had not before writing.

However, these are people who often, probably usually, already have a deep knowledge of what they are writing about and a depth of vocabulary to bring to the task. For students who struggle with writing, this is rarely the case. Often, these struggling students have limited knowledge in particular and limited language in general. For them, conversation with other people about what they will write, especially guided conversation, is a critical step in building meaning *before* writing. It is a step which has frequently been omitted in the writing classroom.

- *We disagree over the role of structures.* Some teachers, particularly those who work largely with expository writing, have placed a great deal of importance on the structures of writing—sometimes so much that the structure becomes the most important feature of the writing. Other teachers, however, have been suspicious of giving students any specific structures. They feel that structures (like the five-paragraph essay) are inherently "formulaic" and ultimately limit a student's own inventiveness and creativity. Out of this fear, teachers have sometimes refrained from giving students any structures at all to follow, trusting that they will come up with a structure that works for what they are trying to say.

  For students who have read a lot of expository text and have unconsciously internalized some of those text structures, this minimalist approach has sometimes been successful. Students without this type of prior knowledge and unconscious understanding, on the other hand, have often floundered as they have tried to build a piece of writing with no internal road maps to follow.

- *We equate "engaged, authentic" writing with writing about one's own personal experiences and/or prior knowledge.* It has long been a truism that one should write about what one knows; all writers know this, all teachers of writing or teachers who use writing in their classes know this. This truism has often led, however, to the idea that one should write about only what one already knows, or at the very least decide for oneself about what to learn and write.

  One of the unintended consequences of this assumption has been that teachers have frequently not paid sufficient attention to how students actually acquired the knowledge about which they would write. In writing from personal experience, the knowledge could be assumed; after all, the knowledge was the writer's own life events or ideas or reflections.

  Because of this emphasis, *the corollary to "writing about what you know" has frequently not been articulated—that you should "know about what you write."* As a result, deliberate, intentional planning for knowledge building has not often been a part of the writing teacher's approach.

Writing for Understanding

Writing for Understanding is an approach that recognizes (like NAEP and others) that *at the heart of effective writing, by any accepted definition, is the building of meaning and expression so that others can follow the writer's thinking.* Therefore, *Writing for Understanding* postulates that if students are to write effectively and with engagement—during testing, for their own personal growth, for school, for real life—they need to have certain elements in place. These elements are:

- *knowledge and understanding which can be articulated in spoken and written language*

- *an appropriate focus for thinking about and synthesizing that knowledge and understanding*

- *a structure through which to clearly develop and present that knowledge and understanding*

- *control over conventions*

In this approach, then, teacher "backward planning" becomes critically important. Before sitting down to write, the student needs to have all of the above elements in place—especially the first three. The teacher, therefore, needs to plan for instruction that will help the students to gain access to each one of those elements.

Conceptually, that teacher planning in the *Writing for Understanding* approach includes the following components:

Planning Components of *Writing for Understanding*

Central Ideas

What is it that I want students to understand about this *content* (and what misunderstandings might I need to address)?

What understandings about the *craft of writing* do I want them to develop?

How will I plan backward from my goal to design instruction so students can get there, and how will I know when they've got it?

Focusing Question

What question will I pose so that students can see how to approach this thinking and writing in a specific, appropriate, manageable way?

Building and Processing Working Knowledge

How will I make sure that students know enough about this subject by the end to actually be able to write about it? How will I make sure they know about the craft of writing?

- What will they read, and how will I help them read it?
- What vocabulary do they need?
- What do they need to draw or make?
- What experiences do they need to have?
- How will I engage all students in purposeful conversation in order to build knowledge/understanding?
- How will students select from and analyze the knowledge through the lens of the Focusing Question, then capture it in notes or some other type of visible thinking so that they have access to ideas to use in their writing?
- How will I monitor their developing understanding so I am sure they are getting it? How will I give them feedback as they acquire and develop that understanding?

Structure

How will students know how to construct this piece of writing so that their thinking is clear, both to them as writers and to the readers of their work?

- What will I show them as a model?

- What tools will they need?
- What concepts of craft will they need to understand and use in their writing?

Writing

How will students draft and revise so that their final writing is clearly focused, organized, and developed to show understanding of the central ideas?

- Again, how will I monitor their writing so I am sure they are getting it?
  - How will I give them feedback as they write and revise to show that understanding?

After planning and instruction that addresses these components, the teacher looks closely at the resulting student work. What did they get? What did they not get? Where is the understanding strong—where is it weak? What transferable writing tools have the students gotten from this that they'll be able to apply more independently next time—and what transferable writing tools still need more work?

After that—more planning. Using information gained from the first pieces of writing, the teacher plans the next unit of instruction that will include writing. Working with the idea of a "gradual release of responsibility," the teacher decides where students still need very direct guidance and instruction, where a little less.

Writing for Understanding and Independence: What's the Relationship?

Ultimately, the teacher is planning so that, both now and down the road, students will show solid understanding of their subject in effective writing. The *Writing for Understanding* approach is based on the idea that students *will come to expect to understand what they are talking about, and will expect to be able to write clearly about it.* It is about giving them an approach and transferable tools, skills, and strategies—not rigid structures or some sort of lockstep procedure—for seeking and building and expressing that understanding in writing.

Writing as a Set of "Transfer" Skills

Several years ago, when we had begun to be highly intentional about *Writing for Understanding* instruction with our elementary- and middle-school students, we happened to run into one of our former students, now a ninth grader in high school. She had been a motivated, strong student, so when we asked her how high school was going, we were taken aback by her answer.

She frowned. "Well," she said, "I just had to write a history paper that was hard. At first I couldn't really do it."

This was distressing to hear. "Why not?" we asked her. "What didn't you know how to do?"

"Oh, I knew *how*," she replied without hesitation. " I just didn't know *enough*. I didn't, like, understand the stuff. So I had to do that first. Then I could write it okay."

"Good," we said. "Good for you." We could not have asked for more (Hawkins 2006).

This ninth grader had come to a place in her writing that we wish for all our students. She had written many essays, reflections, research papers, and narratives in which she had constructed real meaning, real understanding. She had learned how to express that understanding clearly in focused, organized, effective writing. When she read her own writing back to herself, it made sense.

Making sense in writing was now an expectation in her head. When faced with a writing task as a high school student for which she was not yet prepared—when she "didn't, like, understand the stuff" —she knew what she had to do. And, in her own words, once she had arrived at a greater depth of knowledge and understanding, she had the writing skills to call on so that she "could write it okay."

What is it that we want our students to be able to do with writing? What does "being a writer" look like? If genuine mastery of a complex ability like writing means being able to *transfer that ability to new situations*, what skills and habits of mind must the successful writer develop?

In *Writing for Understanding*, we have identified this critical set of skills and habits of mind:

Control over elements of written expression. First, writers who are comfortable in a new writing situation, with new demands, are familiar with and have appropriate control over elements of written expression. Even young writers in the early grades use skills and craft. As they get older, their tools become more sophisticated, but regardless of the age, a student who is a writer is able to use skills and craft flexibly and appropriately. These include the elements of effective writing we read about earlier, described by NAEP and agreed upon by the writing community everywhere.

Habits of mind. In addition, writers who are comfortable facing a new writing challenge have certain habits of mind. How students approach the writing task (or any task) matters. Teachers have long known from empirical experience that a student's attitude towards learning, as well as his or her orientation to learning, make a huge difference in how well or how poorly that child learns. In writing, our experience has shown us that two habits of mind, in particular, make a difference in how well students transfer their learning to new, more independent writing tasks.

The first is *expectation of meaning.* When students have written many pieces over the years that make sense and reveal understanding, then they come to expect all of their writing to reflect similar sense and understanding. They do not settle for "sort of" getting it. Students who are accustomed to meaning-making and understanding in writing know from experience when they understand a subject well enough to proceed with the writing. And they know when they need to help themselves in some way, perhaps by re-reading, by gathering more information, or by further discussion.

The second is being *"learning oriented."* This is an approach to learning, or in this case to writing, whereby students view a writing challenge as a problem to be solved, as opposed to a set task which has a solution that is either right or wrong (National Research Council, 2000). In our experience, students of any age who transfer successfully, in writing, view the writing challenge as one which they are capable of meeting. They are willing to persist to some degree until they have, if you will, solved the problem. Being learning oriented in writing involves an attitude of competence, a willingness to persist flexibly, and an adequate ability to self-monitor one's thinking and writing.

In our experience, these skills and habits do not usually spring up spontaneously in students, especially in struggling students. Rather, *they develop as a result of many successful experiences with thinking and writing.* As we break down the elements of backward designed planning that make up the *Writing for Understanding* approach in the following chapters, it will become easy to see how students become more and more able to transfer their learning about writing in both of these areas.

**Towards Independence: The Role of
Embedded Instruction in Reading**

In the world of reading instruction, the last few years have seen a surge of interest in how to help students comprehend what they read. Recognizing that reading comprehension is, in fact, what reading actually is, teachers have searched for ways to help students become able readers. They have searched for ways to help students become readers who can navigate many kinds of text and who have the tools, or strategies, to make meaning out of that text, even when the text is difficult.

As those strategies have been identified and broken down into skills (activating prior knowledge, finding the main idea, questioning, predicting, and the like), there has sometimes been a tendency to expect students to abstract these skills very quickly. If we give students lots of practice in "finding the main idea," the reasoning sometimes goes, they will be able to transfer that skill to, say, reading a primary source document like *The Federalist* or the description of a set of symptoms for a complicated disease. If we do several exercises with predicting, we hope, students will be able to transfer this abstract skill to reading *Crime and Punishment*, or their science textbook, or the consumer report on the recall for their car, or a presidential candidate's position on protecting the environment.

In fact, however, giving students fragmented "practice" in reading strategies does not help students very much. They do not become more capable readers.

Over the past few years, researchers have made some discoveries and developed some insights into learning and the ability to transfer knowledge to new situations—in short, to solve new problems. It does not come from being a sort of generic "good thinker" or a "good problem solver." Rather, it appears to grow from a deep familiarity with a particular body of knowledge. Only when people have that deep knowledge base are they able to form general principles and concepts, which they are then able to transfer to new situations and new demands (National Academy of Sciences, 2000).

In the world of reading instruction, this understanding about learning means that students are far more likely to become capable, strategic readers if they are learning reading strategies while in the process of acquiring deep content knowledge. The National Reading Panel states that "when the strategy instruction is fully embedded in in-depth learning of content, the strategies are learned to a high level of competence" (Rand Reading Study Group 2002). In other words, students use reading strategies to build specific content, or domain, knowledge and understanding. When they have repeated, successful experiences with this, they are far more likely to abstract those strategies and apply them independently to new situations.

Building on this insight, the 2004 *Reading Next* report states that, if we are serious about helping our struggling adolescent readers with reading comprehension, one of the essential components of the curriculum is that instructional reading strategies be embedded in content area instruction (Alliance for Excellent Education, 2004).

Towards Independence: The Role of Embedded Instruction in Writing

We have found that the need to teach skills by embedding the learning in the deep consideration of content is just as true for writing as for reading, perhaps even more so. Students will not learn to write by being taught abstracted elements like "details" or "voice." Even if instruction is broken down into smaller components ('introduction" or "transitions" or "show, not tell" craft lessons), students cannot and will not become effective writers if this kind of instruction occurs in a fragmented or decontextualized state. Writing absolutely needs these and other skills, but it is much more than a set of separate skills. Just as students will not learn to read capably across a wide range of texts and in a wide range of situations if they are given only abstracted skill lessons in the absence of deep, coherent content consideration, so they will not learn to write thoughtfully if they are taught only discrete, abstracted skills in the absence of deep, coherent content knowledge. In our experience, students need to be helped, over and over again, to experience what it is to write thoughtfully, clearly, and with solid understanding.

Just how much is "over and over again"? How much practice do students really need—all students, not just the advantaged—if they are going to be competent, independent writers at their grade level—or as adults? And what kind of practice?

There is no easy, "one quantity" answer to this, of course. Perhaps the best way to think of it is in terms of other skills that take practice. A basketball player does not expect to dribble expertly or make great lay-ups on the basis of a few gym classes or sessions on the neighborhood playground. A piano player does not expect to be able to play Mozart's "Minuet in G" or a Scott Joplin rag after a few runs through the sheet music. A parent does not want his son or daughter getting behind the wheel of a car after a single highway experience. Developing competence in any of these fields requires much practice.

Further, the practice is not limited to a series of drills or skills sessions, though it surely includes that. Rather, the young basketball player has many experiences with whole games, with another team opposing his and the opportunity—in fact the necessity—to think on his feet, to monitor what he is doing, and to adjust as he goes. He is building meaning of the game. The piano player, even at the most basic level, does not just play scales or finger exercises, though those surely matter. Instead, he plays whole pieces frequently—first with one hand, then with two, then with chords—building meaning of the music. The young driver practices putting in the clutch, operating the hand signals, and parallel parking with a sawhorse, but she also drives on the road, with other drivers, in real traffic —building those skills within the overall context of actually driving. In each case, the learner is putting discrete skills to work flexibly, as needed, to build meaning.

Writing for Understanding is built on these principles. Knowing what they want students to be able to do in the end—create written products that make sense and convey meaning to both writer and reader—teachers plan backward so that students have plenty of knowledge and guidance and practice in getting there, including plenty of opportunity to write whole pieces that make sense. Their instruction takes into account the need for students—all students—to expect to understand what they are writing about and to have tools of written expression to demonstrate and develop that understanding.

Below is an example of a social studies teacher's backward planning for her upper-elementary students. The students will be writing about the Christmas Truce of World War One, an event in which both German and British soldiers all up and down the trenches of the Western Front put down their guns and treated each other like brothers.

Sample of *Writing for Understanding* Plan: *The Christmas Truce*

 ### Central Ideas

Content: People's beliefs can influence their behavior in extraordinary ways.

Writing: To write effectively in response to text, we choose evidence from the text thoughtfully and explain its relationship to the focus of the writing.

Focusing Question

How did the arrival of Christmas Eve affect the fighting in the trenches of the Western Front in December, 1914? Why?

Building and Processing Working Knowledge

In order to gain sufficient knowledge to be able to address the focusing question, students will have these learning experiences:

- use atlases to identify countries involved in WWI
- map the Western Front, share photographs of no-man's-land between trenches
- listen to an article on The Christmas Truce read aloud to them
- partner-read the article
- confront focusing question, "How did the arrival of Christmas Eve affect the fighting in the trenches of the Western Front in December, 1914?"
- as a group, develop focus statement in response to question, something like "The arrival of Christmas Eve caused the troops on both sides to treat each other with friendship and good will." This focus statement will serve as the controlling idea for the writing.
- in pairs, go back to text, paraphrase evidence from text to support focus, put on graphic organizer note templates (visible thinking)
- in pairs, share evidence on note templates, discuss as we go

Structure

- supply students with one model paragraph which includes context, paraphrased evidence from notes, explanation relating evidence back to focus; work with model paragraph in discussion

- remind students of structure they have already used in writing responses to text (summary intro, focus, body paragraphs with supporting evidence, conclusion)

Writing

- have students write summary introductions in class, share before going on
- continue writing in class, stopping to share and get feedback on body paragraphs with evidence and revise along the way
- stop for discussion again before writing conclusion so all students have a chance to process the "so what" conclusion ("So, what does this event show about the power of belief systems to influence people's behavior?")

In the next chapters, we will take a closer look at each of the planning and instructional stages in *Writing for Understanding*.

TO SUMMARIZE....

- There is widespread agreement on the elements of effective writing. These include establishing a purpose and focus, developing a structure, including details and development, and using conventions accurately.

- Even though there is an implicit recognition of the role of knowledge and understanding in effective writing, the effort to ensure that students develop that knowledge has often been overlooked as part of writing instruction. Just as it is important for students to write about what they know, it is also important for them to know about what they write. *Writing for Understanding* builds this critical element of planning for content understanding into the teacher's backward design planning.

- When writing instruction is a part of content instruction (as it is in reading instruction), students are more likely to internalize the lessons of good writing and ultimately become able to transfer those writing skills and habits of mind to new situations.

- Students who have frequent experience with creating writing that shows understanding are more likely to expect to build understanding when they write in new situations.

Section II

Teacher Planning
for Effective Writing

Chapter Two:

Planning for a Focus

Writing for Understanding is based on the idea of "backward planning." What does that mean?

In real life, we use backward planning all the time. If an overloaded parent knows he has to be at the soccer game at 3:30 to watch his daughter kick off, he plans the rest of the day with that very important outcome in mind. He doesn't leave getting there on time to chance. The very busy parent knows he has to pick up the dry cleaning first, and he has to stop at the supermarket to buy pretzels for after the game. Allowing for traffic, he has to leave work by 2:00 to get all those errands done, so that at the opening whistle, he is there in the stands, cheering for the team.

The Problem: Lack of Intentional Planning for Writing

In education, we have often not been particularly intentional about planning to achieve specific student understandings—at least, not in the world of content writing instruction. We have been far more likely to say, "I want my students to write about the Civil War" than to say, "I want my students to show they understand that the Civil War affected North/South relations for the next century in a variety of ways." As writing teachers, we have been far more likely to say, "I want my students to write about their reading" or even "I want my students to be able to use the writing process" than we have been to say, "I want my students to show they understand what a caring elephant Horton is in the Dr. Seuss books and to be able to organize those ideas clearly."

Some ten years ago, Grant Wiggins and Jay McTighe articulated a paradigm for intentional planning and teaching called *Understanding by Design* (Wiggins and McTighe 1998). Its premise is that *effective education is all about deep understanding.* According to Wiggins and McTighe, we as teachers need to be clear with ourselves about identifying the understandings that we want our students to reach and then intentionally plan our instruction, backward, so that students arrive at them.

This concept of "backward design" underlies the principles of *Writing for Understanding.*

The Solution: Designing Backward for Focused, Effective Writing

With the help of teachers' thoughtful, intentional, backward planning, students can learn to write effectively. We have found that approaching this planning within a series of questions and steps can be very helpful to teachers and their students.

Designing Instruction Backwards: The Importance of the Central Ideas

Planning for Understanding Content Information and Ideas

When a teacher plans a unit that will include a piece of meaningful writing, often culminating with that writing, the first "central idea question" he asks himself is about the content itself. This consideration includes:

- "What do I want students to *know* about this topic by the end of the unit?"

- "What do I want them to *understand* about it?"

- "What might that understanding reasonably look like in a piece of writing at this grade level?"

A question often arises here: just how big does this central idea need to be? The answer, as in so much else about writing, is "it depends." In life, we need to write for all kinds of reasons and to construct and show all types and levels of understanding. The same is true for school. *Writing for Understanding* needs to be, and is, a flexible approach.

So the central idea might be very big indeed ("war causes suffering") or it might be smaller ("monarch butterflies have an amazing life cycle"), or something in between. What is important is that the teacher know what central idea, what understanding, he is after and plan so that all students have access to the knowledge that allows them to reach that understanding and communicate it appropriately in writing.

Planning for Understanding of the Craft of Writing and its Elements

The second central idea question the teacher asks himself is about the writing skills. These include:

- "What elements of writing (skills and craft) do I want my students to work within this piece of writing?"

- "What elements of writing (skills and craft) do I want them to take away—or at least to begin to or continue to internalize—from this work?"

Again, the writing skills addressed will vary with the lesson, with the students, with the purpose. In any piece of writing, the successful finished piece will show the elements of writing, "the grandmother of all standards": a focus, developed through a clear structure and supported accurately and thoughtfully with details (see Chapter One). However, within these elements, teachers will plan for different central ideas about writing. A *Writing for Understanding* sequence of instruction may focus on learning to use transitions, for example, or it may emphasize using parenthetical citations in a research paper. Whatever it is, that "central idea" about writing is part of the teacher's backward planning.

Planning for Understanding Reading Strategies

Often, depending on the grade level and the topic, there is also a central idea for reading. The teacher might ask himself:

- "What reading strategies do I want my students to work with in acquiring the content knowledge and understanding they will need to be able to write effectively?"

- "What strategies do I want my students to use in gaining this knowledge and understanding for writing? What strategies do I want them to practice?"

As with planning to develop content knowledge and writing skill, teachers sometimes plan for certain strategies, skills, and habits of mind related to reading within an overall *Writing for Understanding* plan. Recognizing the interdependent relationship between reading, speaking, and writing, and knowing that reading comprehension strategies are best internalized through constructing meaning in particular content, teachers will often include attention to particular reading strategies as part of their overall "backward designed" plan. A central idea in reading for a second grader might be "reading the text again and again is helpful"; for a fifth grader, it might be "paraphrase! paraphrase!" Again, whatever the reading skill or habit is, it often becomes part of the teacher's *Writing for Understanding* instructional plan.

The Focusing Question. Closely related to identifying the content-related central idea that the teacher wants students to show in writing is crafting the focusing question. This is the question that the teacher will pose to the students to focus, prod, or shape their thinking and writing. *If having a focus is the key to clear student thinking and writing, then it is essential that the teacher design an effective focusing question.* Through the focusing question, the teacher helps students to narrow their exploration of information and ideas through the close consideration of this single question.

Depending on the unit, the grade level, the level of understanding the teacher is seeking, or many other factors, the focusing question will vary greatly. A kindergarten teacher working with the poem *Us Two*, in which Pooh and Christopher Robin spend the day together, might use a very specific and concrete focusing question like "How can we tell that Pooh and Christopher Robins are friends?" A high school history teacher working with the Constitutional period might ask, "How are Hamilton's and Jefferson's differing views of human nature reflected in the Constitution?"

In both cases, the teacher crafts the focusing question to help the student think about the text or the body of knowledge under consideration in relation to the overall central ideas. The question might point students toward developing a piece of writing that shows a basic understanding of the text or body of knowledge. On the other hand, it might point students towards developing a piece of writing that shows a more analytical, inferential, even evaluative level of understanding. That decision is up to the teacher, who knows his students, his curriculum, and his reasons for teaching this particular text or body of knowledge.

Inside the Classroom: Two teachers plan for the central ideas and the focusing question

Because *Writing for Understanding* is useful at all grade levels, let's look inside the classrooms of two teachers at different grade levels, one a first-grade teacher and one a middle-school teacher.

Primary Response to Literary Text

A first-grade teacher wanted to help her students learn to think critically about what they read. She was working with understanding character as an important way to understand text (even in first grade!)—a concept that will ultimately help students understand many texts. Knowing that her students responded well to the rhythm of poetry, she decided to use a short poem as a text to use as a basis for a written response to text at a developmentally appropriate level.

On the following page is one student, Olivia's, final piece of writing.

Clearly, this first grader has produced an effective piece of writing. What kind of planning did the teacher do that ultimately enabled this child to produce this written response to text? Specifically, what central ideas was she after, in terms of both content understanding and writing skills?

Let's take a look at the teacher's thinking.

"I know I want my students to be able to make inferences about character when they read (there's a big concept for you!). We've

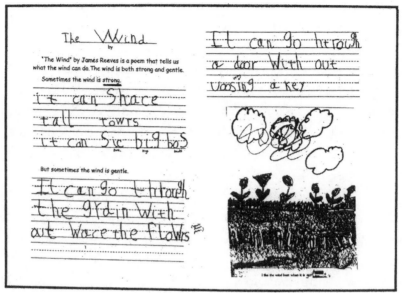

Vermont State Benchmarks, K–4, 2002

been doing a lot of that in our reading instruction, especially our read-alouds. We discussed how curious Goldilocks is when we read Goldilocks and the Three Bears, and we found evidence for that by going back into the text.

"Oh, and we decided that Mrs. Mallard is a good mother when we read *Make Way for Ducklings*—we found lots of evidence for that when we went back into the text.

"So, now that I think my first graders are familiar with the thinking involved in making sensible inferences about characters, I'd like to try having them write a response to text that demonstrates that kind of thinking and understanding of reading. They also get the idea of going back into the text to support their inferences, and we can build on that growing ability.

"Hmmm... let's see. This poem, 'The Wind' by James Reeves, is a great one. Look at that imagery. It's almost like the wind itself is a character. When I read the poem, I see that the wind is pretty complicated, even though the poem is so accessibile to young children. It's strong, but it's also gentle.

"That's the central idea about content that I want them to pull from this poem—the wind is both strong and gentle. So the focusing question I need to pose to them is pretty clear—'In this poem, what is the wind like?' If I want to give them even more support (and I think I do, since I want to make sure every student is successful with this writing), I could ask, 'How is wind both strong and gentle in this poem?'

"Of course, I also want these first graders of mine to gain experience with a fundamental concept about writing—that, to show good thinking, they need to go back into the text to find good supporting evidence for their ideas, for their focus statement. So that's my 'central idea' about writing itself—in writing about text, we support a focus statement with evidence from that text."

This teacher still has planning work to do. But now that she has determined the central ideas she wants students to develop from this piece of thinking/writing, she is well on her way to doing the rest of the planning—and the students are well positioned to be successful when they write.

Middle School Narrative, Social Studies

A middle-school American history class was immersed in a long unit of study on the American Civil War. The teacher had several concepts she wanted the students to take away from their study. One of these was the understanding that this war, like all wars, had very complex and varied effects on people. This was a broad concept that would have much leverage as students continued their study of war over the years and tried to make sense of their own times.

The teacher also wanted students to recognize that in expressive writing, paying attention to tiny details matters greatly. In a narrative, the all-important focus is not a focus statement, as it is in a response to text or a persuasive piece. Rather, the focus for a narrative is the conflict or struggle in which the character is immersed and which drives the action of the story. This teacher wanted students to build on their understanding that all those rich details need to contribute to developing that conflict. The teacher, then, chose that understanding as the central idea about writing that students would explore in the culminating assignment.

She decided to ask her students to write a short historical fiction narrative as a way of constructing and then demonstrating these understandings. Below is the work of one student, Will, written from the point of view of a small Southern child whose home lay in the path of Sherman's March to the Sea near the end of the war.

The Boy

The young boy stood with the most menacing look he could muster spread across his face. He just stood there watching the endless columns stretch as far as the eye could see down the long, dusty road. The soldiers would turn and look as they went by, and he made sure to look right back. He made sure to stare as far as he could into the dark pupils of their eyes, as if it would raise the house that was now nothing more than a heap of ashes. Only a few charred remains of the walls were left.

As his eyes went from soldiers to remains he saw a small soft lump poking up from the ashes. He knew exactly what it was and he turned away. That (stuffed) bear had been his favorite friend. Not a toy, it was more than a toy to him. For a second he was back on a green lawn, with the shutters of a house tapping softly on the window pane. And there was his bear. They waited for the next pirate ship to come around the bend in the road, so they could board it and make the captain walk the plank. But then he heard a shout and knew he was back on the dusty road with no green lawn and no shutters tapping softly.

He leaped down from his perch on an old dresser, one of the few things that hadn't been pillaged or burned in the fire. He bent down, putting both hands on his knees as his eyes searched the ground intently. He picked up the most deadly rock he could find and hopped back up on his perch to resume his watchful glare. No soldier escaped the watchful eyes as they probed them. The giant snake of blue tails was tapering off, and the boy could now see the end of the tail. The boy once again hopped down from his perch. He could feel the sweat-covered rock in his palm. The last of the blue columns were passing.

The boy took a step forward and leaned back, then whipped his body forward and released the rock at the same moment. The boy heard a thud as the rock came home and the rear most soldier clutched his side and looked back—but all he saw were those hateful eyes with tears rolling forth.

How did this teacher begin the backward planning process that led to this task? Let's take a look as she thinks the task through.

"Understanding the complexity of the effects of the Civil War is such a huge task! In fact, understanding cause and effect at all is such a huge undertaking. How can I make the writing task concrete enough so that my students really get it, yet still give them some freedom to approach the idea creatively?

"The other aspect of understanding I want them to have is that this was not just some big, lifeless chunk of history. Instead, these were real people whose lives were irrevocably affected by war. That's really the central idea I'm after here.

"So, maybe a good way to do this is to have my students write a very short narrative. If they take on the perspective of one fictitious person, they can build a concrete, specific understanding of one effect of the Civil War from that person's perspective.

"I'll need to be careful, though. When my students write narratives, it can be hard for some of them to focus them appropriately, and they go on and on, including everything that they've learned.

"So, I think this might be a perfect place for a 'moment in time' narrative, where they choose a tiny moment or event (with a built-in conflict or challenge, since conflict lies at the heart of narrative writing) and a character in that moment. The narrative will show one life being affected by the war, the way that the character is struggling in some way. That'll be the conflict.

"Now, what about those rich details? I have a fair number of students here who haven't read much on their own over the years, and that deficit really shows up in expressive writing. My central idea about writing, then, will be that good writing includes rich detail.

"But there might be a problem here. My students don't have as much language floating around in their heads as some other students might. I think I'll make sure to read lots of models of this type of writing aloud. Then we'll talk about it, so that students can pay close attention to what 'rich detail' looks like. This way, they'll be better prepared when it comes time to really sit down and write.

"Of course, the disadvantage to this whole sequence is that each student is really only looking closely at the effect of the war on one person. When I read the narratives they write, I'll be able to see how their writing is coming along, but I also want to be sure that they understand my central idea about content: that the war affected different people in different ways. I know: if I have them read their pieces aloud together, as they develop them and if we discuss them all along the way, I think they'll get a sense of the complexity and diversity of the effects of the war. I know they love listening to each other's work. And they'll also get some great work with rich language, in a context that makes sense."

This history teacher, like her colleagues, has not completed her planning. But her identification of the central ideas that she wanted students to develop during the unit is a critical step in getting her students to that place of understanding.

The Writer's Perspective

From the student writers' perspective, what has happened in the pieces of writing produced through these units? What has each one learned about the particular content? What has each learned about writing? What has each learned about building meaning?

In some ways, these pieces of writing are the result of very different student experiences. The first-grade sample, a piece of expository writing, shows inferential thinking about poetry and is the result of highly scaffolded instruction. The eighth-grade piece, an expressive narrative, shows synthesized, applied understanding within the parameters of narrative writing.

But in the most important ways, the student experiences in these two pieces are similar. Each piece is a coherent, complete, connected construction of understanding in writing. When the first grader reads her piece aloud to her peers and then to her family, she is reading a coherent chunk of meaning. She has grasped the concept about the wind's complex character, and she has grasped the concept about supporting her focus statement by going back to the text for evidence. In the same way, when the eighth grader reads his narrative aloud, he recognizes a human being, a child who has been hurt by the war and whose world has been altered beyond recognition. And he knows that his readers will gain the same recognition from the focused, rich details in his writing.

Thanks to the clear planning their teachers did when they identified the central ideas and the focusing question for the writing that was to come (as well as the other planned instruction that followed), these students are well positioned for their next piece of writing—and the next one, and the one after that. They have constructed meaning for themselves, and will take that expectation of meaning ("this is what it feels like to understand") to the next writing task. They have expressed that meaning in clear and logical ways that allow other people to follow their thinking, and they will likewise take that idea of focus, structure, and support to the next writing task.

In the next chapter, we will look at the next steps of teacher planning that are so helpful to students in becoming thoughtful, capable thinkers and writers.

TO SUMMARIZE...

- **Backward planning for effective student writing begins with the teacher identifying the understanding she wants her students to communicate in writing—a "central idea" about the content they are studying.**

- Once the teacher has decided on this content central idea, it's important to come up with a related focusing question which will guide students in establishing a clear focus for their writing.

- Since people write for a variety of different purposes, that focusing question can be crafted to lead to a solid under-standing of a range of ideas. Sometimes that idea will be big, and sometimes smaller, depending on the teacher's goal for the sequence of instruction as a whole.

- Equally important, the teacher must define a central idea about writing that students will learn and apply.

Chapter Three:

Planning for Making Meaning: Building and Processing Working Knowledge

So, knowing at last how the Buddha must look, the artist fell asleep and slept for twenty-four hours as though he were dead, while the housekeeper held her breath and the little cat walked on the tip of her white paws. At the end of twenty-four hours, the artist awoke, and, calling hastily for brushes, ink, spring water, and a great roll of silk, he drew at one end the figure of the great Buddha reclining upon a couch, his face filled with peace. The artist worked as though he saw the whole scene before his eyes. It had taken him three days to know how the Buddha should look, but it took him less than three hours to paint him to the last fold of his garments, while the housekeeper and Good Fortune looked on with the greatest respect and admiration.

—*The Cat Who Went to Heaven*, Elizabeth Coatsworth

"We spent a lot of time learning about and discussing what it means to drink responsibly. And the kids had really good notes that we'd taken together, arranged under a focus that they all understood. I couldn't believe it—my most struggling

students wrote and wrote in class that final day, and asked if
they could have more time because they had so much more
to explain."

—Seventh-grade health teacher, Vermont

The Japanese artist in *The Cat Who Went to Heaven* and the
struggling writers in the seventh-grade health class are not
anomalies. They are both examples of what we know to be true
about writing: most effective writing is not something that writers make up or free associate in some way as they go along. Most
effective writing, by the time it is being committed to paper, is
already in fairly clear shape, both in terms of ideas and structure,
in the writer's head.

This is not to say that "writing as discovery of what we really
think" is not real. It is real, sometimes even at the most basic level.
What research suggests, however, is that for "discovery" to happen, writers need to already know a good deal about what they
are saying and have a pretty clear sense of the point they want to
make about it. George Hillocks points this out in his *Research on
Written Composition* (1986). After a discussion of current research
on the composing process, Hillocks writes that "writers do invent
or 'discover' the specific details, words, syntactic structures, and
perhaps some larger structures as they write" (p. 7). He reports,
however, that "the data in these studies suggest that most writers
have a strong conception of what they will write before they begin
writing or shortly after they rephrase the assigned topic."

In other words, student writers who write effectively have a great
deal in their heads when they sit down to write. Like the Japanese
artist and the struggling seventh grader, they have a good sense of
where they are going—a plan in their heads—when they pick up
the pencil or sit down at the keyboard.

The Problem: Lack of Sufficient Knowledge and Understanding before Writing

When students write about personal experience, they are often starting from a knowledge base. If Marianna is describing her grandmother's house, she is very familiar with that house. If Tony is writing about how his puppy's death affected him, that is an experience which is a part of him.

In content writing, however (and sometimes even in personal writing), this strong grounding in knowledge is frequently lacking. A third grader writing about *The Cricket in Times Square* may not have been able to read the book well. A seventh grader writing to persuade readers that cell phones are dangerous may lack any statistics regarding cell phones and accident or illness rates. A tenth grader writing about the role of the Tenth Federalist Paper in ratifying the Constitution may not really understand either the Tenth Federalist or the Constitution.

In cases like these, with vague or incomplete understanding of the content, students cannot have a reasonably clear sense of what they will say before they sit down to write. How can they plan to show understanding in writing of something they do not, in fact, understand?

For teachers, then, the challenge seems clear: what kind of planning can we do so that, when students sit down to write, they have a clear sense of what they know and where they are going with the knowledge and understanding they have?

The Solution: Plan for Building and Processing Working Knowledge and Understanding for Writing

We have already discussed the importance of articulating the central idea that teachers want students to be able to explore effectively in their writing. What happens next? How do teachers plan so that students will know and understand the information and ideas that they will be writing about?

A brief word is in order here about the distinction between "knowledge" and "understanding." Clearly, the two are intrinsically related, and the distinction is not a black-and-white one. In general, however, we are using the terms in this way:

Knowledge is a set of basic building blocks. Knowledge refers to concrete, relatively small units—the math facts, what cows eat, what the term "evidence" means, where one can find a good deal on snow tires. It is helpful to think of knowledge as being binary: either a student has it, or he does not. It can be transmitted easily from teacher to student or from text to student.

Understanding reflects a synthesis, even an application, of knowledge. While not necessarily huge, it is a joining together of smaller units of knowledge—the understanding that counting by ones and by tens is similar; the understanding that if there is not adequate rainfall, the cows will not have enough to eat in the fall; the understanding that one always needs evidence to support a point one is making; the understanding that snow tires will make a car more stable on winter roads. Unlike knowledge, understanding exists along a continuum. One student might have a naïve understanding of an idea, while another might have developed a more sophisticated understanding. And unlike knowledge, understanding cannot be easily passed from teacher or text to student. Understanding must be earned, over time, by the student, as he considers information, makes connections, and asks questions about what it all means.

In *Writing for Understanding*, teachers plan for students to gain both knowledge and understanding—*knowledge* because it underlies understanding, and *understanding* because that is what real, transferable learning requires. It is what effective writing demonstrates.

Designing Instruction Backward: The Importance of Working Knowledge and Understanding

There are many ways that people acquire knowledge. At its most fundamental level, knowledge comes from direct experience. An urban child can speak knowledgeably about city blocks and subways. A rural child can speak knowingly of mud season and farm fencing.

However, to write effectively, students have to be comfortable with working with knowledge *in language, in words.* When Hart and Risely published their much-heralded study several years ago describing the 30,000,000-word gap that exists between disadvantaged children and highly advantaged children *entering kindergarten* (Hirsch 2003), alarm bells went off in the education world. Although the numbers were shocking (30,000,000????), the truth those numbers pointed to was not. How would it ever be possible to help those children become literate students and adults, to say nothing of helping them become effective writers? How can one write in the absence of adequate language?

There is no question that the gap between the advantaged and the disadvantaged is profoundly troubling. However, individual teachers, and sometimes whole schools, have found that it need not be a permanent sentence of "forever behind" in terms of writing. Intentional planning for specific content knowledge, expressible fluently in language, is key.

In this chapter we look closely at the elements of planning and instruction in *Writing for Understanding* that give students access to specific content knowledge that they can express in language. It is these elements that teachers need to build intentionally into their planning so that, by the time students are sitting down to write, they can *use that knowledge to develop understanding and build genuine meaning with their writing.*

Our experience shows that planning for students to gain sufficient content knowledge and understanding requires teachers to pay attention to several elements that might, at first glance, seem to be separate issues. These critical areas include vocabulary, reading comprehension, and oral processing.

Vocabulary. Clearly, vocabulary is the essential building block of language. This fact seems so obvious that it does not even bear repeating, yet it is something that we have often not paid attention to. A student cannot make sense of reading when he is unfamiliar with many of the words and concepts in that text. He certainly cannot use them to create meaning, for himself or for a reader.

Think again of the young author of "The Longest War." She is trying to write about freedom, yet she appears to have only the fuzziest ideas of what "freedom" means (in addition to having misinformation about who won the Vietnam War). The author of "Catwings," on the other hand, has a solid understanding of the word "similarities" (even if he cannot spell it!). For both of these writers, control of specific vocabulary is essential if the writers are, first, able to understand the content they have studied and, then, write with understanding.

When a teacher is planning for writing, then, he plans intentionally for *specific* vocabulary acquisition so that students can control the information and ideas that they must master and work comfortably with the focus of the writing. Which concepts and words will writers need to grasp adequately? Which concepts and words will they need to hold in their heads as part of the prewriting plan, if they are to write effectively? How will the teacher make sure they master the key vocabulary and, thus, are able to focus on their writing?

Reading comprehension. In school and in life, students gain a great deal of their information from reading. The writer of the League of Nations piece had to read about World War One, the Treaty of Versailles, and the League of Nations. He had not acquired this knowledge as part of his general background knowledge domain. The writer of "The Wind" needed to be able to read the poem she was writing about. She needed to be able to connect that knowledge to her own experience to be able to make sense of it—to understand it—so she could write about it.

Vocabulary knowledge is clearly an essential component of reading comprehension. Reading experts point out that if students are to understand what they read, they need to know between 90 and 95% of the words in a text (Hirsch, 2003). This is one reason the 30,000,000 word gap has such mind-boggling implications.

Students also need to be able to read fluently if they are to pull meaning from what they read. Again, reading experts agree that, in general, if children cannot read a text fluently (defined in words read accurately per minute, with phrasing), they are unlikely to pull meaning from that text—too much of their "head space" is devoted to figuring out the words to be able to also think about the overall meaning (Hirsch, 2003; Allington, 2001).

This could be a spot where the 30,000,000 word gap might appear to present a formidable obstacle. For the middle school or high school teacher, the challenge can easily seem insurmountable. How can a teacher "fix" the gaps that exist, not only from early disadvantage but now also from years of struggling or failure in reading in school? How can a sixth-grade teacher teach children to read?

It seems important not to discount how very large this challenge is for teachers, especially teachers who see upwards of 100 students per day. It is real, and it is daunting.

But the good news is that it is not insurmountable. Research is showing that "reading comprehension strategies" are most effectively taught *in the context of learning a body of content knowledge* (Snow, 2002). In other words, the science teacher who is planning for her students to use a specific vocabulary to write about the parts of a cell, helps them to reread and paraphrase, *within the context of specific texts*. She does not set out to help students' reading comprehension in the abstract. She does not simply distribute a vocabulary sheet and ask students to memorize the definitions. Rather, she uses specific texts that use the vocabulary in context, texts that require students to understand the meanings of the key terms in order to understand the ideas developed in the texts that they are reading. And she works with them to help them gain comprehension from those texts.

For the student who is going to have to gain knowledge from what he is reading in order to be able to write, the challenge for the teacher is clear: how will I plan so that my students are able to understand *this text*? What kinds of techniques will I use—read-aloud, repeated reading, reciprocal teaching, visualizing, paraphrasing, summarizing—so that *these texts*—and the vocabulary they contain— are accessible to my students? How will I plan the reading so that students gain the specific knowledge and vocabulary that is required, then hold it comfortably in their heads as an integral part of their overall plan when they sit down to write?

Oral processing of ideas. There are some writers, in our experience, who can work out their ideas so well in their own heads that they can go right from reading (or viewing, or experience) to writing. They can make the overall plan quite independently. In fact, state assessments and other testing situations often demand the ability to do this, so the goal of independently being able to formulate one's ideas into an overall plan is useful.

However—and this is a big "however"—it is our experience that, before students can reach this level of independence in writing, they need to have a great deal of experience with processing their knowledge. They need to talk it, to turn it over, and to examine it with slightly different words or from different angles. They need to engage in conversation where the back-and-forth of ideas helps them to gain understanding of those ideas in their own words and in their own minds.

The work of theorist and linguist Lev Vygotsky (1978) has been illuminating in this regard. All learning is social, according to Vygotsky, and requires language. Writing in the 1920s in Russia, he posited that we learn from our interactions with others, and he formulated the idea of zones for acquisition of learning. According to this theory, all people learn best when they are within what he called the Zone of Proximal Development for any given skill. This zone is the cognitive region where they cannot yet perform a given skill or set of skills independently, but can perform successfully with the guidance and help of a teacher/coach.

In the Vygotsky worldview, teachers hold a crucial place. Teachers are people who operate within the Zone of Proximal Development, deliberately and intentionally creating guided learning opportunities (scaffolding), including and emphasizing and working through language, so that students may eventually reach independence, or the Zone of Actual Development.

Writing for Understanding instruction is deeply indebted to Vygotsky's ideas and principles in many ways. The overall idea of providing deliberate scaffolding to help students write clearly and with solid understanding on any one piece honors his view of the importance of deliberately guiding learning. And the goal that students will eventually become able to transfer the skills necessary for effective writing to more independent situations also grows organically from Vygotsky's work.

For our purposes here, though, let's look at the importance of oral language. Vygotsky was a linguist. He set great store by the idea that to gain understanding of anything—tying one's shoes, cooking a stir-fry, analyzing a text—one needs to use language in a social context. In other words, we learn within the context of conversation. Once we are more sophisticated, that conversation might occur only in our own heads, perhaps with an author (this is what allows a good reader to learn from a textbook, for example). But when we are younger, or working with exceptionally challenging ideas, we need actual, out-loud processing of thoughts, exchange of ideas, conversation, re-working of understanding, in order to gain comprehension and construct meaning.

Arthur Applebee discusses the importance of this oral processing even for university students. In his *Curriculum as Conversation* (2001), Applebee argues that for ideas in curriculum to have lasting, integrated meaning for students, they need to be meaningfully connected and synthesized through thoughtful conversation. He predicates the possibility for this "curriculum as conversation" on two conditions: that the materials the teacher is using actually be thoughtfully chosen and connected, and that real, thoughtful, deliberate, sustained classroom conversation be structured around those ideas. Only when these two conditions are present, Applebee argues, will lasting learning about particular content and ideas take place.

If this is true of all learning, how much more true it has to be of writing! Writing is the synthesized use of connected ideas that have to be expressed in clear language to construct meaning, for the writer as well as for the reader. How can we possibly expect a child, especially a child who struggles with language, to write coherently about specific ideas that he cannot express orally?

Part of the teacher's planning in *Writing for Understanding*, then, is to build in opportunities for students to fully discuss orally the content they will be writing about. This can take different forms: summarizing, dramatizing, debating, "turn and talk," questioning, and more, depending on the students and the content. Regardless of how it happens, though, oral processing is an essential step in producing thoughtful, effective writing. Again, at the risk of being repetitious, if a teacher's long-term goal is to have students transfer their understanding of what it takes to write thoughtfully and effectively to an independent situation, he wants to help them build the habit of working with ideas deeply enough to understand them—and oral language is an essential part of that.

Capturing the knowledge.   The Japanese artist in *The Cat Who Went to Heaven* did not need notes by the time he painted. He had meditated so completely on what he already knew about the Buddha before he painted that he could paint directly, and swiftly, from what he held in his head.

The struggling seventh grader, though, used notes to write. He had an overall sense of what he was going to write. He knew the point he wanted to make. He knew the structure through which he would develop his ideas. And he understood his material. He did not, however, have every statistic committed to memory. He did not have each aspect of each fact memorized.

What he did have was notes. Within his in-his-head overall plan for writing, this young, struggling writer had a strategy for fleshing out and developing his ideas. His notes were tools that helped him produce a solid, clear, thoughtful piece of writing on how to drink responsibly—content which mattered to his health teacher, and to him.

In *Writing for Understanding*, we have found that appropriate notes are essential at all grade levels. We have also found that they can look quite different, depending on the ideas being considered, the developmental level of the students, and the task itself.

For a primary student, notes often take the form of pictures. Pictures selected from a text or drawn by the student himself serve to help the student formulate ideas into words. Pictures serve to jog the memory of the student who is still learning to physically produce clear letters and words on a page. The young writer of "The Wind" is a good example of this. Often, notes are "public."

They might be on the wall, in charts or other forms, for all to see and use. Sometimes, notes are even physical objects that students can manipulate—note cards, icons, even objects.

For older students and adults, notes can also take various forms. Sometimes they are key terms written in the margin of the text with which the student is working. Sometimes they take the form of two-column notes or learning logs or whole-group charts. Sometimes, notes are a list of bulleted ideas, and sometimes they take the venerable and time-honored form of index cards.

Sometimes, teachers plan note-taking in combination with text mapping of various types. We will discuss this form of "visible thinking" in Chapter Four on structures.

In short: writers cannot write about what they do not know. They cannot use words and ideas in writing that they themselves do not understand. Intentional planning for that knowledge and understanding, then, is key to solid *Writing for Understanding* instruction.

Designing Instruction Backward: The Importance of Planning for Knowledge of Elements of Writing

Building knowledge of craft: the elements of writing. Writing, we know, is the construction and communication of meaning. A teacher who is planning for effective writing, then, plans not only for student acquisition of solid content understanding. She also plans for developing student knowledge of the elements of writing. Depending on the task, the age of the students, and the particular needs of those students, the teacher builds into her plan opportunities for her students to gain adequate understanding of the elements of writing. Since every piece of effective writing develops from an appropriate focus and structure, she plans to include consideration of that focus and structure as a part of her instruction. If there are other elements of craft she is working with (perhaps transitions; perhaps use of metaphor; perhaps good leads), she plans to consider those, as well.

What about Time?

Without question, this kind of attention to student knowledge and understanding takes time, sometimes a great deal of time, especially when teachers and students are just beginning working with the *Writing for Understanding* approach. While there is no easy or one-size-fits-all answer to this question, it's helpful to think about several considerations.

- Even without taking writing into account, good teachers agree that students learn more, retain more, and connect to other ideas more when their teachers plan for depth of understanding as opposed to breadth of coverage. Therefore, the "frontloaded" planning that goes into *Writing for Understanding* instruction is really what planning for good instruction looks like.

- Related to this idea is the question of setting priorities. Teaching is a dynamic process. With all good instruction, and certainly with *Writing for Understanding* instruction, each teacher needs to set priorities. Within the curriculum of his school, and with awareness of his state standards, he needs to think carefully about what students need to know and which concepts provide the most leverage to other ideas, then tie writing to those concepts. It will then be worth the time it takes to make sure students can construct and show solid understanding in writing.

- It takes time for people—not just students—to learn something new. When that "something" involves writing, a complex undertaking even for people with a good command of language, ideas, and structures (to say nothing for people who struggle with any or all of these), the time can be significant, especially in the first stages of instruction. Dedicating that time makes sense. As one of us has often said, "You need to go slow in the beginning if you want to go fast later on."

- If a teacher's goal is to have all students experience successful, thoughtful writing (and ultimately transferable skills in both understanding and writing), then time is required throughout the process. If the teacher gives short shrift to the instruction for student understanding or for writing skills *before* writing, then he will have to put in the time in the form of individual conferences or even individual mini-tutorials *after* writing. Our experience is that it is far more efficient and effective to put in that time before writing.

Inside the Classroom: Two Teachers Plan for Knowledge and Understanding

Teachers in *Writing for Understanding* classrooms, at any grade level and in any content area, pay significant attention, in their planning, to the "building and processing" stage of pre-writing. In the two sequences below, the teachers have already completed their "central idea" planning, so they know the content and writing understandings they want their students to be able to communicate when they write.

Elementary Informational Writing, Social Studies

A third-grade teacher was planning a whole-class, standards-based unit on the Abenaki, a native group of Vermont. This was a curricular unit that the teacher knew was important and would take several weeks. Within the unit, he planned to have the students do several "shortwrites" in the form of journal entries, summaries, and little responses.

But he also wanted students to think critically about what they were learning. He had chosen the central idea that he wanted students to share in writing, that Vermont's geography had a big effect on the way the Abenaki lived. This concept, he reasoned, was important in itself. It also was a state standard, and it was an idea that would have a great deal of leverage for his students in the future. The concept of the relationship between culture and geography is one which contributes to people's understanding of the world in which they live—not only historically, but in the present. If students could build understanding of this in the context of their study of the Abenaki, they would be working with a critical thinking skill that they could begin to transfer to other situations.

The teacher also knew that it was important to make that concept of the relationship between geography and culture accessible to students in a concrete way. Keeping this in mind, the focusing question he had developed for the writing was, "How does the land affect the way Vermont Abenakis lived?"

One of his third-grade students, Teresa, has worked hard to develop her literacy skills and crafted an effective piece of writing. She wrote the piece after a multi-week unit, intentionally planned so that all students would be solidly familiar with the necessary information and ideas, including specific vocabulary and information, and have a clear structure within which to express them.

The Abenaki lived all in Vermont. They were Indians who lived in the 1600's. They moved around for hunting, fishing, and gathering. Vermont's land affected the early Abnaki's food and their clothing.

The Abenaki used the wildlife like turkey, deer, and moose to feed the Abenaki family. The women gathered plants, berries, nuts, roots, bulbs, leaves, flowers, seeds and grasses. The vegetation was gathered, eaten, planted and made into food baskets. The Abenaki used tree to make maple syrup. They colekted sap from the trees.

The land not only affected the food, it also affected the clothing of the Abenaki. The Abenaki used the wildlife like bear, deer, moose, and beaver hides and fur were used to make clothing like breech coats and moccasins. The Abenaki used shells and bones to decorate their clothes. The Abenaki used birds feathers for headdresses for special occasions.

In conclusion, the food and clothing were affected by the land. The Abenaki used nature to keep them alive.

Another student in this class, Barry, also wrote an effective piece.

The Abenaki lived in Vermont in the early 1600. The Abenaki are a group of native people. They lived here much before you and me they learned how to dell with the land. There were no houses no electricity not even heating the land had hills mountains lots of trees rivers. Vermont's land affected the early Abenaki's housing and their food.

Vermont's land affected the Abenaki's housing. The Abenaki used young trees to build their houses. They cut it down and then bent it into a round roof. This kept the Abenaki warm in the winter because the roof kept the warmth in. Vermont's land also had lots of animals. They skinned the animals and took their sinews the sinews held the saplings together. This helped the Abenaki keep their houses stable. Vermont's land also had lots of trees. They used the bark from the trees to tie on the frame like s(h)ingles. That helped the Abenaki keep the rain out so they staid drie all the time. The Abenaki's housing was affected greatly by the land.

Not only does the land affect the Abenaki's housing but it also affected the Abenaki's food. The Abenaki women picketed seeds in the forest. Then they planted them in some fresh soil. This helped the Abenaki because they had their own gardens and they planted the seeds and soon they had food. Vermont's land also had a lot of fish. They killed the fish and the dead fish helped fertilize the soil. That gave the Abenaki extra food. Vermont's land also had abundant wildlife. The Abenaki fished and hunted game. All of the fresh meat was shard among the whole village to keep everybody strong. The Abenaki's food supply was affected by the land.

Vermont's land affected the early Abenaki's housing and their food. The land seems to be a tough place to live, but the Abenaki respited (respected) the land and only took what they needed and the land gave them what they needed.

Both of these pieces of writing show clearly that the writers understand the central idea, at an appropriate third-grade level, as did the other young writers in this class. Barry's piece is more developed than Teresa's, with a more precise vocabulary and a more thoughtful conclusion. But both writers clearly understand the concept that the teacher had identified, and express that understanding effectively in writing

What kind of planning did he do so that these students would be able to successfully write these essays? Let's take a look and see.

"Let's see... I'm really asking these kids to think in terms of cause and effect here. Do they really get that? I think I'd better make up some sort of activity that zeros in on cause-and-effect thinking—maybe a game. If we can play that game with something they already know, hopefully they'll be able to think in terms of cause and effect with this new information they're going to be getting about Vermont's land and about the Abenaki.

"Okay, so far so good. Now what about the information? I have several books that I think will be useful. Some of them are library books—I'll read those out loud. I also have a few short texts with multiple copies that we can all read. One is hard, I know—I'll need to make sure the students get to hear that one aloud first before they read it to each other. And I have those wonderful Abenaki folk tales—they'll be great as a literary source for kids to draw knowledge from.

"Oh, and they need to talk. That will mean lots of guided discussion—oh, and I have a reader's theater play about Abenaki life. Perfect! They love acting, and it's a great way to get them to work with the ideas over and over without getting tired of it.

"Now...there is going to be a LOT of information...I need to have a good way to keep track of it, stay very familiar with it...I want to make sure the students get very familiar with the information on both Vermont's geography and the Abenaki, so that the cause-and-effect connection can be really clear for them. I think I'll make a big chart on that wall by the flag... we can use it for 'public notes.' I can have the kids draw pictures of the geographic features of the land, and also pictures of the Abenaki using those features to get their food, their transportation, and so forth. That will help with the vocabulary, too—some of this vocabulary is fairly specialized."

This third-grade teacher has figured out ahead of time what he will do in class, including the materials and processes he will use, so that his students can develop a solid understanding of the ideas they will be working with when they write. He is using the principles of *Writing for Understanding* in a developmentally appropriate way. Like the teachers in Chapter Two, this teacher still has some planning to do, most notably planning around direct writing instruction. But with the planning he has done, his students—including the hard-working writers whose work we read—will be well prepared to write with understanding.

Middle School Response to Text, Social Studies

A middle-school teacher was planning a unit on the complex forces that come together to create history in general and specific historic events in particular. She had already decided that the central idea she wanted her students to grasp from this study was a broad one: history is not simple and should not be oversimplified. She also wanted them to understand that large forces like economics, geography, technology, human desire for power, and human values and beliefs play a large role in the way historical events unfold. She also understood that this central idea was very abstract and that she would need to offer concrete information to her students if they were to begin to grasp it.

For this sequence of instruction, the teacher decided to use the article "The Long Night of the Little Boats" by Basil Heatter, the story of the rescue of the British soldiers stranded on the beaches of Dunkirk during World War II. The focusing question that the teacher posed for writing was, "How did the forces of history come together in the rescue of the British soldiers at Dunkirk?"

Here is one student's response. The author is a sixth grader, Tonya, who has worked hard at writing. After much class discussion, she wrote this piece independently.

The Night of Little Boats

The story "The Long Night of the Little Boats" tells the story of little boats rescuing stranded soldiers. At the beginning of the story British troops got cornered by the Nazis in Dunkirk, France. Somehow word got out to England that their troops were stranded in Dunkirk on a beach. England immediately got a big group of people together from all walks of life to take on the challenge to save their troops from the Nazi grasp. They gathered boats of all kinds to sail over to Dunkirk to save their troops. Meanwhile, in Dunkirk their troops were being bombarded by the German Nazis. The English troops started to lose all hope until the little boats came and started ferrying the soldiers home. While the boats continued their efforts to save soldiers, the Nazis studied ways of attack. Yet fighting the time, thousands of English soldiers were saved. As the Nazis saw the last of their prey escaping, the Germans made one final bombardment of bullets and bombs. Finally the skirmish was over and the little boats saved over 335,000 soldiers, as they only hoped to save 30,000.

In one event, we can see the broad forces of human history have come together to make it happen. Three of these forces would be Technology, Values, and Geography.

First, Technology played a big part in the story "The Long Night of the Little Boats." When the English troops lost hope of ever getting rescued from the German Nazis, the little boats came to save them. The little boats worked all night ferrying soldiers safely to their home country England. The technology of the little boats helped the English save their soldiers from the German troops. If it wasn't for the little boats 335,000 soldiers (or) more would have died from the Germans grasp. Another time technology played a big role is when the little boats sailed to England. The English had car tires on board to fend off any artillery that would come their way. Car tires helped fend off bullets and bombs. They also helped save lives. Now you can see that technology played a big part in the story.

Next values played a big part in the story. Values played a big role when the soldiers were stuck on the beach. Englishmen did whatever they could to save their fellow soldiers' lives. This shows values because the English were valuing their soldiers by trying to save as many of them as possible. Again values is shown in the story when the English sent brave-hearted men to got to rescue the troops that were cornered on Dunkirk, France. The story says, "But most of them had just their brave hearts" to save their troops. This shows values because if it wasn't for the brave-hearted almost none would have shown up to rescue the English soldiers.

[The writer goes on to explain the role of geography and concludes by restating her focus.]

The next piece comes from the same class (a multi-grade, middle-school class). This writer, Peter, is an eighth grader who participated in the same discussion as Tonya. Peter also wrote independently.

The Miracle of 1940

Human history can be complicated. When we look at any big historical event, we know that there can be many causes. Great forces are at work, often all at the same time. The same can be true of even smaller events that don't have an effect on a large amount of people.

In the story "The Long Night of the Little Boats" by Basil Heatter, we learn the story of how British troops were stranded in France and rescued by a bunch of small boats run by locals. It was 1940, and the Nazis had cornered most of England's troops on a beach in Dunkirk, France. In England, the government heard about this. They then issued an announcement saying that all owners of small, self-propelled boats should come help. They did. All sorts of people, rich and poor, rose to the challenge, because they wanted to save their troops. Boats of all shapes and sizes made their way across the English Channel at night towards Dunkirk. They arrived just in time, because when they got there, the Germans were bombarding the British. As each boat got to the shore, they immediately began loading the very orderly troops onto their boats, then went away from the shore to bring them to the bigger boats that were making their way up the coast. The Germans, sensing that they were losing their "prey", redoubled their attack on the English. The British soon realized they were fighting time as well as the Germans, because when dawn came, the Nazis would see everyone without the use of flares, and pick off all the troops at will. When the little boats loaded the last of the troops and ferried them away, the Germans let out a finally barrage of artilleries. At last, the English were able to count the men they had saved, which turned out to 335 thousand, even though they planned to save only 30 thousand.

In this event, we can see that the broad forces of human history have come together to make it happen. Three of these forces would be desire for power, geography, and technology.

The first force that affected this bit of human history is desire for power. Desire for power is a strong, apparently insatiable, need to control or have authority over others, which had become quite common among men at that time, one of them being Hitler. When the boats were in the middle of rescuing soldiers, they weren't intimidated by the German's display of destructive power, and didn't give up the struggle. The reason they made this decision is they didn't want their country to end up like the rest of Europe, which was invaded by the Nazis. As a result, they fought back against the Germans most vigorously and aggressively, which the rear guard of the British demonstrated. "The exhausted crews looked toward the beach and saw only a handful of men left—the soldiers of the rear guard, who were still firing at the advancing Germans." This vigor that the soldiers showed also allowed the boats to save more men.

Even though the Nazis had control of most of Europe at that time, they still wanted England in their control. This is why they didn't allow the English to escape easily and without many losses. You see, they really didn't want them back in England. The troops that were on the beach that night were the greater part of the British Army. The Nazis knew that if they got back to England unharmed or without a lot of their number depleted, they would fight back against any attempted invasion. They also knew if they were the victors of that night it would possibly discourage the rest of the Army back in England. As a result, the little boats had a tough time, racing back and forth between the shore and large ships, which caused them to break down....

Peter continues with a deeply developed analysis of the roles of both geography and technology in the rescue of the soldiers at Dunkirk. He concludes by writing,

(All) of the impacts of these forces led to the boats saving more British soldiers than expected. It seems that they have turned that night in 1940 into an event that people will talk about and no one will forget for ages and ages.

Like the third-grade writers, these students show a clear understanding of the central idea: the role these forces played in this particular event in history. While the second piece is more sophisticated than the first in both ideas and language, each writer shows a good grasp—in clear writing—of the impact of the forces of history in shaping this particular event.

How did the teacher plan to make sure her students understood these ideas? Let's follow her thinking.

"There's *so much* to learn about history (as my principal used to say, 'Why would anyone want to teach history? There's more and more every year! It never gets smaller!') I do know that I want to make sure my students recognize that human history is not simple... that's my central idea. I want them to get lots of opportunity and practice in thinking critically about human events, both in the past and as they happen around them—and teasing out multiple causes and multiple effects is a big part of that. So is seeing patterns.

"At the same time, I know that these concepts are tough! I think they'll be able to get 'technology' pretty well—but values? Economics? Even geography?

"So, I clearly need to start with making sure students have an adequate understanding of those terms. We'll gather lots of examples of those forces, then generalize from those to come up with definitions that are as concrete as possible. I think we'll also do a drawing display of graphics of these terms for the classroom wall, so we can refer to it as often as we need to.

"Now—the 'Little Boats' article itself. It's hard in some spots, with lots of complex sentences, so it will be a challenge for some students to read independently. Still, it's so dramatic—I think even my most concrete-thinker students will get pulled into it if I read it aloud to them first. Then I'll have them work in pairs to read it aloud with each other before we summarize as a group. Maybe I'll use a reciprocal teaching approach to that reading.

"In any case, that group summarizing will be important. I want to make sure they have really synthesized the key ideas about the event before they have to try to analyze it in terms of the forces of history. I'll see how well they can manage this synthesis on their own (they've written quite a few summaries before), but I'm going to check these 'little boat' summaries before we go on to the analysis.

"Then what? How do I make sure they really get to work with those hard, abstract concepts in *this context* so that they know what they're doing when they write? First, I think I'll guide them through a partial third read, and we'll gather notes on 'geography' in this event together...and maybe strong ideas and beliefs. I'll make a graphic organizer for this. I want them to get it well. Then they can take the rest of their notes with their partners—that will give them plenty of time to talk and go back to the text (which I know they'll have to do a lot).

"Is that enough, though? These are such abstract ideas, and I'm asking them to juggle a few of them at the same time. Well, I do have all those new colored pencils...maybe if I give each student five tagboard circles (the base of that vase will be just the right size), they can create a drawing of the way each of these concepts shows up in the article. They'll work in partners, of course, and then share their drawings, explaining in words, in a class circle. That way, I'll be there to help guide the conversation if I can see some misconceptions popping up. And both the tagboard circles and student notes on the class discussion will provide helpful records of the information, so the kids have access to it for writing.

"Oh, my gosh—I can see that this is going to take a lot of time. Well...so be it. I want to make sure every kid in this class is successful...and I know they *can't* be successful if they don't have a really good grasp of these ideas."

This middle school teacher has planned for understanding. The student engagement with the ideas resulting from that planning will stand the teacher and, more importantly, the students, in good stead.

Like her third-grade colleague, however, this teacher is not finished. Students will need to know how to "build" the piece of writing—literally, how to construct their knowledge and present it clearly so that others can follow their thinking.

The next chapter will address how to build this into planning.

TO SUMMARIZE....

- **Many problems in writing are really problems in understanding: students often know little about what they are trying to write.**

- ***Writing for Understanding* emphasizes teacher planning for students to acquire knowledge about content, which includes attention to reading specific texts, working with specific vocabulary, engaging in much discussion and other types of oral processing, and 'capturing' the knowledge in note form. All of this preparation is in place to ensure that when students come to write, they know what they are writing about and can begin with a clear plan for the writing that has already come together in their heads.**

- **In addition to specific content knowledge (knowledge students will need for this particular writing piece), teachers plan for knowledge of craft—the elements of writing students will need to be familiar with for this particular piece of writing.**

Chapter Four:

Planning for Structures in Writing

Oh, somewhere in this favored land
the sun is shining bright;
The band is playing somewhere,
and somewhere hearts are light,
And somewhere men are laughing,
and somewhere children shout,
But there is no joy in Mudville—
mighty Casey has struck out.
—*Ernest L. Thayer*

Once upon a time there was a girl named Karen. She had always wished to be a princess. She wished of having royal food and wearing beautiful clothes, but most of all she wished to have a room of her own.

For she lived in a small house, so she had to share a room with her two sisters, which she dreaded most of all, for they laughed when she told them what she wished for....
—*Meg, Grade 2*

"So, let me get this straight—you're asking us to write
to persuade...so that's write an introduction, give a thesis
statement, support with true information, use a counter-
argument, and finish with a conclusion—right?"

—*Luke, eighth grade student, having been given an*
assignment to write a persuasive essay

Structures are so deeply and fundamentally a part of what we
as human beings do and think that we often do not even recognize
them. The pattern of the final lines from "Casey at the Bat" sets up
the reader for the joy that others are feeling, in contrast with the
sorrow of the great Casey striking out. Second grader Meg opens
her tale with "Once upon a time," a pattern familiar to both her
and her readers. It gives her, as the young writer, a way to begin and
signals us, as the readers, that a story is unfolding. When Lucas, the
eighth-grade writer, clarifies his task, he is repeating for himself
the overall plan for what he needs to do to develop his ideas.

Each of these writers has used, or will use, a familiar structure
to make and communicate meaning. At the same time, each has
used it flexibly, to fit his or her needs, first to envision the overall
thinking, then to move along clearly to the next idea, and the next,
so that the whole thought has meaning—first for the writer, then
for the reader.

Why Do Structures Matter?

Ideas cannot exist, or at least they cannot be named, without
shared language. By the same token, connected ideas, ideas that are
more than simple names or actions, cannot exist without shared
structures and patterns.

In the past few years, a great deal has been learned about how
the brain organizes ideas and information into chunks, using pre-
existing patterns, so that the individual is able to make meaning.

Briefly, we recognize that "mental models," or schemata, are the foundation of cognitive growth (Clarke, 1990; National Research Council, 2000). Simply put, "schemata are unconscious mental structures assembled from past experiences that we reapply as general frames in trying to make sense of new experiences" (Clarke, 1990). It now appears that some mental models, or schemata, seem to be intrinsic to every developing mind, while others are acquired over time as we come to understand certain domains (say, the way car engines work) and certain approaches to critical thinking (say, how to consider two sides to an issue before arriving at a position on it). In any event, mental structures are now recognized to be a critical feature of cognitive growth—of learning, of understanding, of constructing meaning.

Writing for Understanding recognizes this truth about thinking. Giving students clear structures, therefore—to help them construct meaning for themselves, and then to communicate that meaning to readers—is an integral part of teacher planning in writing instruction.

The Problem: Disagreement over the Place of Structure in Writing Instruction

Within much of the world of writing instruction over the past thirty years or so, there has often existed anxiety or sometimes even outright hostility around the deliberate teaching of specific structures to students. The concerns seem to have centered around two issues: the potential of structures to restrict or constrain student writing, and the potential for structures to lead to rote, formulaic thinking. Because each of these concerns is so important, we want to address them briefly here.

Structures as restriction of student freedom. If we look briefly at the course that modern writing has taken over the past hundred years, it is clear that writers have often tried to rethink old forms.

As novelists and poets have responded to the challenges of their age, they have tried to break various molds, to create new forms and structures as part of expressing new ideas and new ways of making meaning of the world. The work of James Joyce, Ernest Hemingway, the *New Yorker* short story, and many others all reflect this hunger to create new forms as an important part of the creative process in seeing more deeply, more truly. This breaking of structural boundaries has been true of academic writing as well. Even science writing, perhaps the most traditionally structured of all writing, has seen an attempt by writers to experiment with different forms as a way of explaining the truth as they see it in a more accessible way. The work of Stephen Jay Gould and John McPhee comes to mind here. In short, the freedom to experiment with form, to tweak pattern, to create whole new structures has been seen as an essential aspect of human freedom and growth.

What seems to have been forgotten here, however, as this idea has been applied to children's writing, is that these writers and mold-breakers were working from structures and schema and mental models that were already well in place in their own minds. Like good jazz musicians, who create embellishments and new expressions from a solid grounding in melody and harmony and rhythm, they were creating new forms from a foundation of recognizable ones. Indeed, much of the writing about freedom for children to create their own structures has been done by people who themselves have a very clear sense of effective expository structure, which they use well to get their point across in their writing! In short, clear structure was essential to these boundary-breaking writers in their creative process. Without it, there would have been no foundation, nothing from which to grow.

Structures as a reflection of formulaic thinking and rote learning. One of the most impassioned arguments that teachers sometimes make against explicitly teaching structures to students is that it creates "rote" thinking, "formulaic" writing. This argument seems to associate instruction in specific structures with student passivity, with simply following a form that has been imposed on them by someone more powerful than they. Such imposition, critics argue, prevents students from thinking for themselves.

It is easy to see where this fear comes from. Anyone who is old enough to remember writing before the writing process revolution remembers that writing could be a pretty black-and-white, rote-learning affair. We remember teachers of writing for whom correct grammar was, in fact, everything. What one said or thought did not really matter. What did matter was how correct the grammar was, whether a modifier was in the right place, whether the comma should really have been a semi-colon. In the primary grades, young children were not doing any writing-as-thinking. Instead they were focusing solely on handwriting, the formation of letters, and the proper spelling of words.

We might also remember a time when critical thinking was not particularly valued. There were certain stock interpretations of texts, of historical events, and of scientific processes. Our job, as student writers, was to give back those stock interpretations (or more likely short answers that show knowledge or the lowest level of understanding) in a clearly articulated, grammatically correct way. At its worst, this kind of writing was in fact much like Pete Seeger's "little boxes"—they were often "all made out of ticky tacky" and they often looked "just the same."

This problem seems less a fault of the structure of the writing, however, than of the thinking that the writer is doing. A structure is a vehicle for thought. If what is asked for is basic recall knowledge, or shallow thinking, then the writing will reflect that. Writing is about thinking. To equate structured writing, even highly structured writing, with shallow, vapid, inaccurate or simplistic thinking, or with a bland or monotonous voice, is to muddy the waters of the nature of truly effective writing. Blaming structures for sloppy or simplistic thinking, or for a lack of effective craft, is like blaming the Constitution for a bad President.

The Solution: Teach Structures as a Matter of Equity

In view of this argument, it seems fair to say that, far from being merely restrictive, structures are essential to making meaning in writing. In writing, structures are not sufficient for effective writing, but they are a necessary foundation. Structures give students (indeed, give all of us) a way to organize experience and make meaning from that experience and to communicate it effectively with others. They do not absolve students from thinking, nor do they guarantee clear and honest thought. Only the writer's intentions, in the presence of solid knowledge and understanding, can do that. What having a structure can do is to free the writer to think deeply and clearly. Just as fluency and vocabulary knowledge allow a reader to concentrate on making meaning out of text, so flexible structure allows a writer to build coherent written chunks of meaning.

Beginning writers, or any writer working with a new genre and new knowledge, can indeed sound clunky, awkward, even tedious. The structure itself in a novice's piece can seem obvious or overbearing, not yet graceful. The same is true of beginning basketball players, beginning knitters, beginning Spanish speakers. When a structure is new, it does not yet flow with the smoothness that it will acquire later.

But to deny a student instruction in structure is, in the end, unfair. It may be that a select few of our students will finally figure it out on their own. (After all, this is what most of us teachers had to do!) If these students read enough of *other people's* clearly structured and thoughtful writing, the theory goes, if they have enough thoughtful conversations, they will absorb structures and build them into their own schema so that they are able to use them flexibly in their own writing. In this view, the teacher simply needs to stand aside and let the magic of absorption happen. And for some students, it does.

However, in our experience, that magical transformation will rarely occur for educationally disadvantaged students, or even for many ordinary students. They are much less likely to absorb those structures from what they read and, therefore, have much less access to structural tools for building their own understanding in written language—or even in thinking. To ask these students to figure out structures on their own is to fail to give them freedom. In fact, it is a hidden form of disempowerment for the very students who need the most help.

For these reasons, *Writing for Understanding* makes instruction in structures a fundamental part of teaching, ensuring that all students have the tools, ultimately, to construct meaning thoughtfully in writing. It is too important to be left to chance.

How Can Teachers Address Structure within Writing Instruction?

There are many ways to help students learn to use structures for organizing their thinking in writing. Here, we will discuss three that have been particularly important and useful: the study of models, the creation of graphic organizers, and the use of a basic essay structure called the Painted Essay.

Models. We sometimes hear teachers express concern over the use of models in teaching writing. Sometimes, they fear that giving students models will encourage them to imitate rather than create, to copy rather than think for themselves.

While it is certainly true that any approach can be misused, we have found that using models thoughtfully is of great help to students. Further, it is a practice widely used in all sorts of instruction, all sorts of apprenticeships. A basketball coach would not think of trying to explain dribbling to a novice player without first showing him what dribbling looks like. A woodworking teacher would not ask an apprentice to make an end table without first showing him what an end table looks like. A math teacher would not expect fourth graders to do long division without showing them the algorithm for it.

Is this imitation? Is it copying? Of course it is, because imitation is part of learning. But as the young woodworker grows in skill, he begins to use those table-making skills in his own way, with his own designs. As the math student grows, he applies his long division skills to his own problem-solving processes.

In much the same way, a teacher operating within the *Writing for Understanding* paradigm would not ask a student of any age to write a response to text or a persuasive piece without first making sure the student had a model of what the end product looks like. *Writing Next,* a report published by the Alliance for Excellent Education, lists "the study of models" as one of eleven elements of writing instruction shown by research to be effective in improving the writing of adolescents (Writing Next, 2007).

A model is more than a visual of a structure, though it includes that. Rather, a model is a completed, coherent body of thought. In a good model, the student can see an idea that has been thought through and developed clearly through a well-formed structure or pattern.

Writing for Understanding teachers begin most writing assignments with a model. This model is usually fairly short and of a cognitive complexity similar to the piece students will be writing. Some models are the work of professional authors, others come from students, but most are written by the teacher to highlight particular skills or concepts. Together, the class analyzes this model. What makes this a good piece?

As the teacher works with the class, she is helping her students see that there are definable qualities that effective pieces share and that these key dimensions of writing can be identified and learned. She may, for example, use state writing rubrics to focus this work, as we do in Vermont. "The Six Traits Plus One" or holistic assessments would work equally well. Together, the class examines the purpose, organization, and use of language and detail in the piece.

Most importantly, the teacher helps the students to see the ways in which these elements work together to create meaning in a piece of writing, the ways in which it communicates clear and connected thinking. Once studied, this model will remain in the student's notebooks all year, as a reference piece. It will be one of many pieces and activities that lead students to develop their own set of flexible, internal structures for purposeful writing.

The next step, especially with younger writers, is often to create a model by doing a group write. The purpose of the group write is to offer students the opportunity to apply what they've learned to a supported, effective piece of writing. Teacher and students write together as a class, on the overhead projector or on chart paper, stopping to discuss the process and decisions as they create. Often, the teacher models how to turn students' suggestions and offered ideas into clear sentences, guiding students in formulating ideas into clear language. These collaborative pieces are "think-alouds" that help students more deeply understand how written language works and will eventually lead to more independent efforts.

This type of support is a hallmark of the *Writing for Understanding* approach. We have found that "…what a child can do in cooperation today, he can do alone tomorrow" (Vygotsky 1962). "Group write" focuses on how the parts of a written piece work together to convey meaning. It becomes yet another model students can use to refine and deepen their schema for effective writing.

Eventually, students are given a writing task that requires them to have internalized and generalized the concepts presented by the model and to demonstrate that understanding in an original piece. Some children cleverly and effectively adapt what they have learned right away. Most, however, begin by writing pieces with obvious, but appropriate, similarities to the model. This appearance of mere imitation may at first be disconcerting, but it is important to remember that, as in Meg's "Princess Karen" story, this imitation is usually a sign of learning. Remembering that all schema begin imperfectly, we do not expect all students, even middle- or high-school students, to immediately apply what they've learned in a sophisticated way. Rather, we recognize these imperfect, sometimes awkward first steps for what they are—the first steps in acquiring tools and habits of mind that they will eventually be able to use in flexible ways and for their own purposes.

Graphic organizers: visible thinking.   Once students have a good sense of a model, of what persuasive writing or response to text can look like and how it works, they can often benefit from using a graphic organizer. Over the past few years, many teachers have discovered the value of graphic organizers of one kind or another. These can range from generic webs (main idea and supporting details, etc) to templates in which part of the piece has already been written and the student is supplying certain parts of the writing to contribute to a full piece.

Graphic organizers can be useful in keeping a student focused in a way that will help him produce clear, thoughtful writing. Generally, we have found that they are not a substitute for a model; if students do not carry a clear, familiar model in their heads (and probably in their notebooks), they will not get much help from a graphic organizer. But once the model is in place, graphic organizers can form a very useful bridge for students to their own writing. They function as a way for students to map their thinking, to establish relationships among their ideas, and then to have a written record of those relationships before they begin to write.

Writing for Understanding teachers call this "visible thinking" and find that the use of visible thinking and mapping in general serves two purposes for students. First, it helps students keep track of the information they are gathering, as well as collect and refine their ideas. Keeping notes has served the time-honored purpose of helping writers remember all the information they want to include and all of the points they want to make. Graphic organizer maps serve this purpose for students admirably, by providing an easy and logical format for record keeping.

Second, visible thinking helps students to clarify and refine their ideas, often helping them to analyze the information with which they are working. Graphic organizers help students not only collect information, but also to organize it, to separate and combine its pieces, and to see connections that may have remained invisible without the graphic form. In short, it helps them move toward the goals of developing understanding and producing meaning.

In his book *Patterns of Thinking,* John Clarke writes about one specific kind of graphic organizer, the map. He reminds us that "by managing the structure of the map, a teacher can direct student attention toward the relationship that the teacher wants the students to examine." (p. 182) This argument can easily be extended to the use of any graphic organizer. If, for example, a teacher wants his middle school students to think and ultimately write about whether the Industrial Revolution helped or hurt humanity, he can supply a graphic organizer that nudges students to organize their information on two sides of a T-chart, one labeled "helped" and the other labeled "hurt." If a first-grade teacher wants her students to compare two versions of *The Three Little Pigs,* she can create a Venn diagram that guides students to make that comparison.

Remembering George Hillocks' observation that most effective writers of any age already have a fairly clear idea of what they are going to write and what their finished product will be when they sit down to write, it is easy to see why graphic organizers have a part to play in writing effectively.

The Painted Essay. One of the structures most commonly and flexibly used in the *Writing for Understanding* classroom is the Painted Essay. The Painted Essay was developed by Diana Leddy, an elementary-level teacher who has taught many grades, including kindergarten. This experience has impressed upon her the great value of making things concrete, colorful, and manipulable so that children can understand what might otherwise be abstract concepts.

The Painted Essay was created as a tool for teaching students about the relationship among the components of a well-written piece. It combines a traditional writing form—the basic essay—with color, activity and oral practice, and it uses different colors to represent different parts of an essay. The different colors help make concrete and visual for students the basic concepts of expository writing: introducing and maintaining a focus, providing supporting detail, transitioning between ideas, and concluding. (See the color insert for a sample of the Painted Essay.)

The key to understanding this graphic lies in knowing, as most elementary students do, that blue and yellow make green. Notice how the green focus, for example, breaks down into two related supporting points—colored yellow and blue. In proof paragraph one (painted yellow), the first (or yellow) point is stated, explained and supported. In proof paragraph two (painted blue), the second (or blue) point is stated, explained and supported. A blue and yellow striped transition reminds the students of the need to move logically from one point to the next. Finally, in the green conclusion, the focus of the piece is restated and reflected upon. In Diana's class, students will actually mix the yellow and blue paints to create this green, reminding them that all of the information in their essay must combine to express their own interpretation of a single idea—the focus of the piece. The shades of green will usually vary slightly, just as students' reflections in the conclusion do.

A word about this conclusion is in order here. We have found that, when children are first working with the Painted Essay or a similar structure, this conclusion is brief. Usually, it restates the focus in some way, with just a bit of the student's own reflection. As students grow and develop, however, this reflection often becomes a deeper level of thinking, of synthesizing. The student's solid understanding, structured to show and drive her internal plan for the thinking, actually leads the student to deeper thinking and understanding. In this way, the act of writing is, indeed, as Hillocks points out, a form of "discovery."

The Painted Essay has proven to be a remarkably useful and flexible structure for students in *Writing for Understanding* classrooms. Although it was designed for young writers in the third and fourth grades, we have seen, over and over again, that students internalize the structure and use its principles in increasingly sophisticated ways as they advance through the grades.

Meg is a student who began using the Painted Essay in the fourth grade. In looking at some of her writing over the years, the "clear thinking" structure that began with the Painted Essay is visible. In one of her early experiences with this format, Meg wrote an essay about a character in a story she had read.

The Master Cat

"The Master Cat" by Charles Perrault, is a story about a cat who helps a Miller's son get rich. The Master Cat is able to succeed because he sometimes acts like a cat and sometimes acts like a human being.

Sometimes, the Master Cat acts like a cat. For example, one time he catches a rabbit to give to the King. Another time he asks the ogre to turn into a mouse and then he pounces upon it and eats it.

But at other times, the cat acts like a person. For example, he goes to the harvesters and says, "If you don't say that the cornfield belongs to the Marquis of Carabas, I will chop you up into mincemeat. Another time he showed his human side was when he gave advice to the Miller's son. Only a person could do these things.

The Master Cat uses both his human and animal sides in this story. He uses his human side for thinking and his animal side for doing the things he has planned. The Master Cat needed both his animal and human characteristics to get ahead.

This piece is a classic Painted Essay. To produce it, Meg has worked with a sophisticated focusing question posed by the teacher: "What makes it possible for the cat to succeed?" She has also worked, in various guided ways, to gain a deep understanding of the text. Both this focusing question and the developing of this understanding were part of the teacher's plan.

Now, Meg uses the structure to think about the two complementary aspects to the cat's character. She has a "yellow paragraph" (acting like a cat) and a "blue paragraph" (acting like a person). In her conclusion, she reflects on why the cat needed both types of behavior.

Now let's fast-forward three years. Meg's seventh-grade English teacher has assigned a response to literature. This piece, on Truman Capote's "A Christmas Memory," while more complex, requires thinking similar to the type of thinking Meg first experimented with in her "Master Cat" piece. Notice the similarities, and the significant differences, in this excerpt from Meg's three-page paper, now that she has several years of experience in writing responses to text.

A Surprising Friend

Often, as human beings, we try to categorize people. We may put people into categories by the way they look or the way they act. Everyone does this, it's how we organize our lives. But sometimes, we are surprised or even shocked by something someone says or does. Just when we think we have a person all figured out... they surprise us! Buddy's friend in the story "A Christmas Memory" by Truman Capote is just such a character. Buddy and his friend live in a house overseen by relatives. The story is set in the rural south in the 1930's and centers around the very special relationship Buddy, a seven year old boy, and his sixty year old friend share during Christmas time. *Buddy's friend is a surprising character because in some ways she is childlike (like Buddy!) and in some ways she is very wise.*

In many ways Buddy's friend is childlike. For example, every year Buddy and his friend make fruitcakes for all of their friends and then celebrate by downing an inch of whiskey leftover from the fruitcakes. Buoyed up by the whiskey, and their own happiness and achievement, they begin to dance and sing around the room. Buddy tells us,

"My friend waltzes round the stove, the hem of her poor calico skirt pinched between her fingers as though it were a party dress: 'show me the way to go home' she sings, her tennis shoes squeaking on the floor"(p. 11)

When Buddy's friend pretends to be wearing a party dress instead of her ratty old calico, it is as if she is playing "make believe"—a game little children play often. The uninhibited dancing and singing also shows her childlike qualities. Most adults would be too embarrassed to do such a thing...

Meg continues to analyze Buddy's friend, giving and explaining evidence to support her focus statement that the friend is both childlike and wise. In her final paragraph, Meg concludes by writing,

...Buddy's friend is one of those people who doesn't fit neatly into a single category. She is full of surprises! These surprising qualities are essential in making Buddy's friend so dear to him. Buddy has a child to learn from and play with, but he also has the wise insight of an adult to help him understand the important things in life.

The language Meg uses as a seventh grader is richer, and both the thinking and the evidence are more sophisticated. But the concepts of writing—the structural and conceptual relationships among the parts of an effective piece of thinking and writing—that she first discovered in fourth grade still hold. Meg has centered her thinking around a clear focus, Murray's "one idea." She then breaks that focus down into related points that a reader can easily understand, supports each point with evidence from the text, and explains the ways in which the evidence supports her arguments.

Finally, with the cueing help of the structure, Meg concludes her piece by synthesizing. She pulls together her thinking and arrives at a deeper understanding of the character and her place in Buddy's life—just as she did about the *Master Cat*.

Several years later, Meg, now a junior in high school, is asked to write a paper on one of the central themes in Homer's *Odyssey*.

The Different Faces of Power

Homer's epic poem "The Odyssey" is the source of many legendary figures of power, both human and divine. At the center of the saga is Odysseus, a man desperately seeking his way home after the end of the Trojan war. The clear figures of power in The Odyssey are the characters that either aid or abet Odysseus in reaching his goal. Homer's Odyssey is a subtle exploration of the nature of power in men and in women.

The Goddess Calypso is one of Homer's powerful characters. Trapped in Calypso's seductive lair, Odysseus's valiant struggles are useless. Our brave hero seems doomed to failure. What kind of a woman has the power to dominate a man of Odysseus's magnitude so completely? The answer Homer gives us is simple—a woman who loves him. Calypso's love is evident in her response when she is commanded to release Odysseus:

"Hard-hearted you are, you gods! You unrivaled lords of jealousy—scandalized when goddesses sleep with mortals, openly, even when one has made the man her husband...So now at last, you gods, you train your spite on me for keeping a mortal man beside me. The man I saved... I welcomed him warmly, cherished him, even vowed to make the man immortal, ageless, all his days..." (5. 130-151)

Calypso is determined to control Odysseus, not from hatred, but from her own selfish passion. Odysseus's brave heart and quick wits stand no chance next to the force of Calypso's emotions. Her irresistible powers of manipulation and seduction are drawn from her love of him.

Another Goddess who greatly effects Odysseus's journey home, and is therefore a character of great power, is the Goddess Athena. Athena takes it upon herself to become Odysseus's personal companion, guiding him through many of the challenges he faces. Although Athena and Calypso seem to be polar opposites, both women have one thing in common —their power emanates from love. We learn of the benefits of Athena's love during a discussion between Odysseus's son Telemachus and Nestor:

"If only the bright-eyed goddess chose to love you just as she lavished care on brave Odysseus, years ago in the land of Troy where we Achaeans struggled! I've never seen the immortals show so much affection as Pallas openly showed him, standing by your father—if only she'd favor you, tend you with all her heart..." (3. 247-253)

Athena's love is enduring and unselfish. She gains control by lovingly guiding Odysseus, rather than the

> more selfish path of seductive manipulation chosen by Calypso.
>
> Athena's love has the power to guide Odysseus home; Calypso's love has the power to prevent him from ever returning. Yet not all of the forces we see at work in The Odyssey emanate from love. When masculine power is introduced into the mix, it's clear that in Homer's Odyssey, love is an exclusively feminine form of power...

Meg continues in this essay with an analysis of the role of power, and concludes by reflecting,

> In his epic poem The Odyssey, Homer explores the nature of power. He examines different types of power, proving time and again that power is drawn from many sources and disguised in many faces. Homer establishes that the root of a woman's power lies in love, while a man's power is derived from his rage. Although power in men and women comes from different sources, all the gods have an equally strong effect on the outcome of Odysseus's journey. It seems that even 3000 years ago, Homer recognized that love can be as powerful as war.

A casual reader may be hard pressed to find the similarities between this excerpt and the "Master Cat" essay, but we can see that clarity of thinking, embodied within a logical structure—including sophisticated synthesizing in the conclusion—has clearly stayed with this student—all the way to high school! Far from being constrained by structure, Meg has internalized it and made it her own.

A caveat is in order here. It is true that the use of models, forms and structures in writing is often misunderstood. These flexible teaching tools have limited value when used *prescriptively or rigidly*. The point of teaching basic essay form is not that all students should always write basic essays, nor that students should follow exactly the form of the model.

Rather, models, forms and structures are best used *descriptively*, to help explain the complex relationship among the purpose, organization and detail of a piece of thinking/writing. They do not stand by themselves but, rather, are used as the starting point for a guided conversation about the qualities of strong writing. They support students while those students are learning about structures, while they are on the way to creating "templates in their heads." When used in this way—to develop abstract understandings about thinking/writing *that can later be applied flexibly*—tools like the Painted Essay are not merely techniques to be learned, they are techniques for learning. In Chapter Six, on transfer in writing, we will see how structure can be internalized flexibly for use in new pieces of writing.

Inside the Classroom: Two Teachers Plan for Structure

Since *Writing for Understanding* teachers recognize the importance of helping students with structure in writing, planning for this instruction is important. Here, two teachers share their thinking about that planning.

Primary Response to Text (Literary)

This first-grade teacher has already decided on the central idea she wants her students to explore in a pair of texts—the idea that two versions of the Three Little Pigs have both similarities and differences. She has articulated the focusing question, "How are the two versions of the Three Little Pigs the same, and how are they different?" and structured the ways in which her students will build the knowledge of the two texts. Her task now is to decide how to give students support in structuring their writing so that they are able to construct and communicate compare-and-contrast meaning of the two texts.

Here is the final piece of one first grader, Josh. (Note: the italicized words were supplied for the young writer.)

The book The True Story Of The Three Little Pigs by Jon Sciesz is about a wolf named Alexander T. Wolf, and three little pigs. There are many things in the book that are the same as the original story, and there are many things that are different from the original story.

One thing that is the same as the original story is there were three houses made by the pigs. One thing that is the same as the original story is the brick house would not fall down because bricks are strong. Another way the story is the same is there is a wolf who blows down the straw and stick houses.

Although there are things that are the same in the two stories, there are also things that are different. One thing that is different from the original story is there was a mean pig who was impolite. The wolf goes to jail because he ate two pigs. The wolf had a cold which blew down the straw and stick houses.

As you can see, there were things that were different and the same.

As a first grader, Josh has produced an effective, age-appropriate piece of writing. He has been able to successfully work with two texts and hold both in his head at the same time so that he can compare and contrast them.

How did the teacher plan so that Josh and his classmates would be able to write effectively? Specifically, how did she plan for the structure the students would use to guide their thinking and writing?

Again, let's listen in on the teacher's conversation with herself as she plans.

"Okay, I know what I want my kids to see here—that these two books have both similarities and differences (and by the way, these students will be asked to write compare-and-contrast essays throughout their school careers, so this is really an important concept). Now, we'll read both books several times. *The True Story of the Three Little Pigs*, by John Scieszka, is so funny—the students will love reading it so often. I think I'll also tell them they're detectives when we talk about the Scieszka book—that always motivates them to listen and read so closely.

"All right—we're going to work with the two versions. I know I'm asking my students to do something different here, and really something harder than they've done before: compare and contrast. Really, that's a complex form of critical thinking for young kids like these, to be able to hold two texts in their heads at the same time, and go back and forth between 'similar' and 'different.'

"When I think about it, that's a pattern I need to help them build. So I think I need to build the structure in at least a couple of places so the students get familiar with this sort of thinking.

"Hmmm.....I know I'm going to use pictures from both texts to create public notes, and the kids are used to doing that. How about if I make two big poster charts, one for 'similar' and one for 'different'? I can make little picture cards for group sorting. That way, when we look at the picture evidence, we can physically put it on the right chart. I think that actual moving and placing the evidence under one category or the other will probably help my students do that kind of thinking (especially my strugglers).

"So, that step will help, but it won't be enough. I think I need to make a second graphic organizer, a kind of writing map, for each individual writer with those two 'same' and 'different' chunks very clearly laid out. Yes, a graphic organizer will work well.

"I'm also concerned that this is a LOT of writing, more than my kids are used to doing. I want to limit the amount of handwriting they need to produce, so that they can concentrate on the actual evidence. This second graphic organizer—the writing map—will help with that challenge.

"Besides that, I want to make sure that nobody is confused. If I include the topic sentence starter and the transitions to new ideas, and leave lines for writing, all the students will have access to this kind of thinking. Of course, some will write more than others, but I think that everyone will be able to do enough to get this. I'll need to make sure I scribe for a couple of kids who will find even this much handwriting daunting.

"It's so important that, when they've finished, they have a *full and complete piece of writing that makes sense,* and that's what the graphic organizer will help them do. The piece is connected, it's complete, it's....well, it's a coherent chunk of meaning (and that's the beauty of writing, once again!). When they read it aloud to each other, it will all hang together."

This teacher was aware of what a "thinking challenge" she was presenting to her students. She suspected they did not yet have a very clear, focused schema in their minds for going back and forth between "similar" and "different." In other words, they did not yet have a firm hold on that structure. Because of this challenge, the teacher made provisions for building the structure, visually and even physically, for and with her students. She supported this effort with a graphic organizer for their writing. As a result, all of her students were able to work successfully with the central idea of comparing and contrasting two texts. Ultimately, they will internalize the structure, "owning" it for later writing they will do, but this is their beginning.

Upper Elementary Response to Text (Informational)

The next two pieces come from a multi-age class that includes grades three, four, and five. The entire class was working with a read-aloud text called *Beatrice's Goat,* the story of a child in Uganda whose family is the recipient of a goat through the Heifer International Project, an international organization that, through the gift of livestock, helps poor families to help themselves. The teacher had chosen this text because her central idea was that "All people around the world need to have their basic needs met."

The teacher knows that this central idea is an abstraction. By itself, as a general idea, it will not have much meaning for her students. But she also knows that through reading and writing about the specific, concrete experiences of Beatrice's family in receiving a goat, her students can begin to grasp this central idea at a developmentally appropriate level.

With those thoughts in mind, the teacher has decided that, for this text, an appropriate focusing question for the entire class will be, "How does the goat change Beatrice's life?" However, knowing that the class is made up of both a range of ages and a range of familiarity with expository writing, she has differentiated the amount of structure she will supply for her students.

The first piece is a group-written piece, with students using a Painted Essay format. The group included mostly third graders and some special-needs fourth graders. This group piece of writing was created interactively, with all students contributing to the finished piece. The exercise of creating this essay gives students the experience of writing effectively, even as they produce this particular piece with a great deal of support.

Beatrice's Goat by Page McBrier is about a girl who lives in Uganda. Her name is Beatrice. She lives with her mom and five younger brothers and sisters. Beatrice's family did not have much money. Getting a goat helped Beatrice's family right away and in the future.

There are many ways the goat helped Beatrice's family right away. One way is when the goat gave birth to twins. Beatrice liked the milk along with her family. Not only did she like it, it gave her family nutrition. Another way the goat helped them right away is they sold the milk for money.

Not only did the goat help Beatrice's family right away, she also helped them in the future. One of the gifts from the goat was money to buy books and a uniform for Beatrice. The uniform allowed Beatrice to go to school. After they sold one of the baby goats, they had enough money to tear down their old house and build a new one with a steel roof. They also had enough money to buy new blue furniture.

In conclusion, the goat helped Beatrice's family right away and in the following months. This story shows how even if your family doesn't have any money or food, your life can turn around by one small gift.

The next piece was written independently by Mike, a fourth-grade student in the same class.

Beatrice's Goat by Page McBrier is about a little girl named Beatrice whos life is suddenly changed to the best by a goat. Beatrice lives in Uganda and belongs to a lucky family who receives a goat from Heifer International. Things were very different for Beatrice and her family before and after Mugisa arrived.

Before Mugisa came Beatrice and her family had no or very little nutrition. This meant that her family was more open to diseases and and not very healthy. Another thing Mugisa changed was their roof. Whenever it rained the roof would leak and they could not afford a new one. Imagine going inside to escape the rain and still be getting wet. Funny to think about but not funny if it happened to you. One more thing that changed was school. Often Beatrice would watch the school children with envy, longing to go, but thinking she never would be able to. Wanting to where a yellow blouse and blue dress studying her school books, but deep inside knowing unless some miracle happened she never would be able to. The other need Beatrice's family needed was money. There family was low on money like most familys around there. They needed money to buy supplies they needed like a new shirt for Moses (her brother) and a new blanket for the bed Beatrice shared with Grace (her sister).

You see now how her life was before Mugisa arrived.

Now (that) you got a taste of what Beatrice's life was like before Mugisa came, I will show you how her life was changed and how different it was when the goat arrived. For one there health and the nutrition of her family changed alot because now they could drink healthy nutrious goat milk. They also could sell the goat milk for money to afford lots of things they need. One especially good thing they could afford was school for Beatrice!! Another wonderful thing Mugisa brought was two kids, Expected and Surprise. They sold Surprise for a lot of money, enough money to knock down there old house and replace it with a new one with a steel roof that would not leak and blue furniture. Now you see how much Mugisa changed Beatrice and her family's life.

Beatrice's life was drastically changed after Mugisa came. I think it's amazing how something as small as a goat can make such a significant change in someone's life.

Like her first-grade colleague, this multi-age teacher knew she had to plan for a structure so that her students would be able to first think clearly about the text in response to the focusing question and then write clearly about it. Her students had worked with the Painted Essay before, but she knew that for many of the younger and more needy students, that structure was not yet sufficiently internalized that they could use it independently. For other students, the Painted Essay was something the teacher knew had been internalized, and was therefore a structure she could expect them to use on their own.

Again, let's take the opportunity to follow her thinking as she planned.

"I know that for my younger and special-needs students, thinking about cause and effect this way is a challenge. They need to hold on to two ideas, the effect on Beatrice now and the effect on her in the future. That ought to work for them. After all, they have done lots of work with Painted Essay structure this year, so they're getting used to the idea of developing a "yellow point" and a "blue point."

"But I also know they're really not independent with that yet. I'm still definitely at the teaching stage with this structure. I do think this group needs to have a few more experiences with being walked through the structure, especially when they need to be thinking in terms of two ideas, "now" and "future."

"I guess, then, I need to help them structure the notes. I'll get some yellow poster paper and some blue poster paper, so as we take the public notes we can very clearly sort the information in the story around which idea they're supporting. This will help them with organizing the information, putting the details on the yellow paper into the yellow paragraph and the information on the blue paper into the blue paragraph.

"So, what about the writing? Well, I think most of these students will do better if we write this one as a group. I'll make a big Painted Essay chart with colored paper and have the kids help me physically select the evidence to write into each paragraph. Oh, and we'll write the introduction as a group first—I know they're still needing help with introductions.

"I do want them to make some moves towards independence, though—it takes so much time and guidance to get there, but I'm sure they can become independent with this structure with practice. I think I'll have them copy over the whole thing in their own handwriting, then read it out loud to people. That way they'll own the writing. I bet the principal would love to listen to these! And maybe the cook! Hearing their own words aloud will help get the complete thought, including the structure, into their heads."

"Okay, that takes care of that group, but what about these older kids, especially the high flyers? I feel pretty confident that these students can use the Painted Essay structure flexibly with this piece. They know about the whole structure—the introduction, the grouping of information, the transitions, the conclusion. And I know we've discussed the text itself, so everyone has a good understanding of Beatrice and the goat.

"So, I think I'll let these kids go on their own and see what happens. After all, if I'm wrong, I can always do some more instructing for the next piece."

This teacher has planned sensibly for structure. Knowing that different students have different needs, she has planned so that students who still need structural support will get it. At the same time, she is planning for the gradual release of responsibility, so that those who have internalized it will be able to apply it flexibly on their own.

The teacher is now ready to plan for the actual drafting and whatever revision students may need and be able to manage. The next chapter will explain how to build these aspects of writing into planning.

TO SUMMARIZE....

- **Giving students clear structures with which to write is important in helping them construct meaning in writing. Planning for structure is an important aspect of the *Writing for Understanding* approach.**

- **Models and graphic organizers of various types are helpful ways of supplying students with a sense of how to structure, or build, a piece of writing that makes sense.**

- **Structures like the Painted Essay are valuable because they provide students with an internalizable, flexible approach to thinking in writing.**

Chapter Five:

Planning for Drafting and Revision

"So, I had this professional children's book writer come and visit my class. The kids loved it. They loved hearing him read, show his drafts of his illustrations, read aloud some of the funny bloopers he had taken out. But then he showed them a big portfolio, and told them, 'See this? These are all my drafts of my book—all fifteen of them! That's right! Writers do lots of drafts before they get what they want!'

I know he meant well, but the kids groaned...I think he had the opposite effect on them from what he wanted."

—*Overheard teacher comment, elementary school*

"Hey, I really zipped right through that piece!"
—*Overheard comment from a student writer*

At this point, the teacher's planning, discussed in the previous chapters, comes together. He has planned for central ideas about content and writing, for a focus within that central idea, for solid knowledge and understanding, for structure. Students will have worked with the ideas so that they are fluently conversant with them, and will have an internal plan for what they are going to write. In a sense, each student will have already done most of the cognitive heavy lifting of the piece of writing, thanks to the teacher's purposeful planning and instruction.

The way the actual drafting happens can and does vary, depending on the age of the students, the length of the piece, the subject matter, the availability of computers, and many other factors. The teacher may ask students to compose in class. He may decide to have them write a section at a time—for example, sharing introductions before going on to the next chunk of writing. Or he may choose to have them write a whole first draft for homework, if he feels his students are ready for that.

Regardless of how drafting happens, teachers in *Writing for Understanding* classrooms find that it often goes surprisingly quickly. If the planning up to this point has been effective, it has paid off. Students by and large know what they are doing. They know how to proceed with a focused, organized, thoughtful plan for their writing. It is a rare child who says, "I don't know what to do," or "I don't have anything to say about this."

But writing remains a challenge. Even when a student has a solid internal plan for how to proceed, even when she knows what she wants to say and how to go about saying it, there is still a difference, sometimes a profound difference, between having a sense of one's message and being able to work it out or express it clearly. Sometimes students are trying out a new element of craft when they write. Sometimes they are working with a new structure. Sometimes they are grappling with an idea that is proving more difficult than they had anticipated. For all of these and many other reasons, writing does not spring forth perfectly from young writers' heads. Students will often find that, on some level, they need to revise. Part of planning for drafting, then, is planning for revision.

We have found that it is helpful to think of revision as a part of that drafting experience. Often seen as a separate step in the writing process (first one writes, then one revises), revision has caused endless angst for classroom teachers. In our experience, it is a rare teacher in a meeting or a professional development session of some sort who does not say, usually in frustration or sometimes even desperation, "I cannot get my students to revise when they look at their first drafts. I can't even get most of them to revise when they confer with each other. *It must be something I'm doing wrong.* The only time I can get them to revise with any value is when I confer with them one at a time, and I just don't begin to have time for that. Help!!!"

In the *Writing for Understanding* approach, revision is indeed an important part of the process of making meaning in writing. It is an aspect of thinking we want all our writers to have and use on some level. Anyone, of any age, who has faced a challenging writing task—whether it is a grocery list for a new and unfamiliar grocery store or a college essay or a PhD thesis—has experienced the need for revision, as well as the sense of satisfaction of having achieved his purpose.

Revision is not, however, an end in itself. Coherence and clarity are the end. Revision is a means to that end, a step on the path to achieving coherent meaning in writing.

Because writing tasks are different, because children are at different age and developmental levels, revision can look very different depending on the circumstances. In the *Writing for Understanding* classroom, however, no matter the grade or developmental level of the students, revision is not an onerous task that makes teachers secretly wish for a snow day. Rather, it is integrated manageably and thoughtfully into the overall plan of helping children write with understanding and clarity.

The Problem: Common Misperceptions about Drafting and Revision

Revision may well be the most misunderstood aspect of the writing process, and often the most frustrating for teachers. Before we go further, it's important to step back and look at some of those perceptions of revision that have given so many well-intentioned people so much trouble.

Students don't revise well because they are unmotivated. Teachers often believe that somehow they have failed to show their students how exciting revision can be, that students do not therefore see the value in revising, and that because of this, they do not revise well (or at all). These teachers believe that if they are positive enough, if they set up enough writing workshops, if they have students writing about what they care about, and if they encourage a "culture of revision," that students will be both motivated about and successful with revision. When many students still fail to revise effectively (or at all), teachers feel at a loss to know what to do.

Revision is where all the real writing work is going to get done. So much emphasis has been placed on revision (peer conferring, many drafts, etc.) that teachers sometimes forget how important the instruction that happens *before writing* or during writing is. When this happens, it is easy for a teacher to find himself with a huge range of instructional needs in the students' writing first drafts, requiring what amounts to one-on-one tutorials if each piece is to get what it needs. Often, this means either that helpful revision cannot happen at all, or that revision takes so long that it is unwieldy or unmanageable.

Revision means writing many drafts. Many teachers believe that it is an article of faith that students should write repeated drafts. They also note, quite rightly, that for young children, who are still struggling with letter formation and transcribing a word at a time, such revision can take forever and become the source of "I hate to write." For older children, who are writing longer pieces, this can also take forever—unless of course the student has very little to say and therefore very little to redraft. In that case, the student measures himself as "not much of a writer," making it unlikely that he will approach the next writing task with much enthusiasm. This is the opposite of motivation; it is a self-defeating spiral downwards for the struggling writer.

Students have the innate capacity to revise, either independently or with other students. In this view, students can do what professional writers do. Since authors, or even very seasoned adult writers, can self-monitor their work, notice what is not working, and work with it some more until it does work, it follows that students should automatically be able to do the same thing. Teachers who believe in this view find it deeply frustrating, especially when working with struggling writers, that students very often cannot self-monitor their work. They often cannot give specific and useful feedback to each other (except sometimes about spelling).

The goal of all writing is to write a polished, publishable piece. This is related to the "15 drafts" notion. In this view, writing should be perfect. Nobody reads published work with spelling or comma errors, or awkward transitions or pedestrian sentence construction. Published work is, at the very least, error free; at best, it sparkles with life and voice. Teachers sometimes think they need to hold students to this "publishing standard" for every piece of writing (which leads inexorably to the "15 drafts" phenomenon).

Revision is an essential, discrete stage in the writing process, and the more one revises, the better. The writing process people (NWP 2006) have long stressed that revision is *not* one of a linear set of steps in composing, but this concept of integrating revision into the whole of writing has not often been clear to teachers. Rather, many teachers have taken revision to mean a discrete step that all writers must go through. Further, they believe that "good writers revise" and that therefore their students will revise every piece —whether they know how to or not, whether they need to or not. Revision is a hoop through which students must jump after a first draft, and the more often they jump through it, the better. Often, teachers note in frustration, such revision is not helpful. Sometimes it is very superficial; sometimes it is fragmented, random, or even counterproductive.

Revision is about "using a writer's toolbox." Teachers know that good writing needs to be engaging for readers. As readers themselves, they know that they are more likely to read and continue reading a text that is lively. Further, they know that there are specific craft lessons—tools—that help build lively and engaging text.

In this analogy, a student writer is much like a cook or a carpenter. It follows, therefore, that students should be able to pick up the writer's toolbox (full of interesting leads, engaging transitions, sparkling adjectives, evocative metaphors), pick out the appropriate tool, and apply it to a revised draft. When, lacking the experience of the cook or carpenter, many students are unable to do this, or to do it purposefully, teachers are disappointed with the results.

The Solution: Rethink the Relationship between Drafting and Revision

How can we redesign the experience of revision? How can we help teachers to plan so that they find revision with students manageable, efficient, and useful? How can we help students to find revision meaningful, even exhilarating—giving them more effective pieces, making them actually more skilled at constructing and conveying meaning in writing, and generating more confidence about their ability to do so?

In our experience, the challenge of getting students to revise effectively is indeed complex. However, at the heart of our *Writing for Understanding* approach lies a view of revision that goes back to the purpose of writing itself—to construct and communicate meaning. Writing is about making and communicating meaning, and revision, on small and large levels, is a form of monitoring and adjusting with the purpose of making that meaning clearer.

Charles MacArthur co-author of *Best Practices in Writing Instruction,* puts this view succinctly. He writes,

> Cognitive models of writing processes describe revision as a process of detecting differences between the intended meaning and the actual meaning. That is, writers have goals and purposes for writing and evaluate what they have written to see whether they have achieved their goals. (MacArthur 2007, p. 143)

In other words, a writer who is successfully revising, monitoring and adjusting his work as he plans and drafts, is working within a plan. He knows where he is going with his ideas and what he is trying to say.

Planning instructionally for revision, then, is part of the rest of the teacher's overall intentional instructional sequence. It is inextricable and inseparable from the planning and instruction that have already gone on. Since revision is about making meaning more clear, it can happen only once students already have a reasonably clear plan for their writing that includes both ideas and the elements of writing: focus, organization, support. In *Writing for Understanding,* that basic plan is the *sine qua non* of writing —including any revision (monitoring and adjusting) that students may need to do.

Connecting Drafting and Revision to Formative Assessment

In the past few years, teachers have heard a good deal about "formative assessment." They know that it grows from looking critically at student work, to see what the student is good at already, what the student is not good at, and what the student needs in terms of instruction in order to move ahead. They know that it provides an opportunity to give feedback so that the student is able to improve.

We have found it helpful to think of revision as a response to a type of formative assessment of writing, at the heart of which is feedback. In this sense, the purpose of formative assessment of writing is *not* to evaluate work in a final sense, or to assign a grade; rather, its purpose is to check in along the way and provide the writer with opportunities to revise as he goes along.

In *Writing for Understanding*, this "revision from formative assessment and feedback" happens on two levels: the student level and the teacher level. The student writer checks in with himself at various points as he writes, getting feedback and assistance as needed. Likewise, the teacher checks in with student writers, formatively assessing for understanding, for development of ideas, for craft—whatever is needed for that particular piece of writing.

Formative Assessment, Feedback, and Revision at the Student Level

Students can formatively assess their writing, with an eye to making it clearer, at all grade levels. Consider the words of two students, below. One is in sixth grade, the other in first.

"I'm writing this personal essay about my grand-mother's death, and I'm not sure if I've told enough about how it affected me personally—can you read it over and talk to me about that?"

—Sally, sixth-grade student

COBRINS

Cobrins is my favrit store in Vermont. you know the state with a lot of farms and dirt roads and big forests and lots of ponds and birds and you know, all that. Now back to Cobrins, now where was I? Oh yaa! I like Cobrins because thats where I ushely spend my allowens. Sometimes in the summer I go there for gum. I like Cobrins!

—Julia, age 6

Both Sally and Julia are doing what MacArthur describes. Each student is formatively assessing her own work in light of what she intends for that work. Is it working? Is it making sense? Then, based on the feedback from that formative self-assessment (in this case, feedback from herself), each student makes a sensible decision. Sally decides she needs some help from a teacher (more feedback!). Julia recognizes that she has veered off course and places herself firmly back within her original plan for her writing.

For both students, that original plan for the writing, which they held in their own heads, was critical—it gave them a clear sense of what to measure their work against, to test both meaning and form.

In contrast, if a student is working with a piece of writing that he himself is unclear about, about which he knows little and whose focus eludes him, it is going to be next to impossible for him to revise that writing in any meaningful way. He cannot formatively assess his work and then make a decision about it because he has no plan in his head to begin with. He has no "intended meaning" against which to assess his writing.

For students in the *Writing for Understanding* classroom, then, revision is often driven by formative self-assessment—not a final evaluation, but assessment in the broadest, most useful sense of that word—against a plan that he understands. *Does this make sense? Can a reader follow my ideas here? Did I prove my point? Am I helping the reader to see what I'm seeing, to feel what I'm feeling, to understand what I understand?*

For most students, especially struggling students or any students dealing with a challenging writing task, formative self-assessment and the getting of feedback—sometimes from a teacher, increasingly from their own analysis of their own writing-in-progress—from that assessment is an evolving skill and habit of mind that takes much experience and much practice. It is not the result of a mini-lesson, and it will not happen overnight. Rather, it requires what the rest of intentional writing instruction requires. It requires genuine attention to knowledge and understanding—no writer can write well, let alone revise, about something he does not know or understand. It requires many opportunities to work with models, and it requires much exposure, both direct and indirect, to specific elements of craft, so that the writer has both a solid sense of possibility and some tools for getting there. It requires many scaffolded opportunities for students to stand back from their writing, mull it over aloud, assess it against specific criteria (including their own focus), share it and chew over its ideas with others, both students and teachers. It requires opportunities for students to make manageable changes in a reasonable amount of time, not to produce a perfect piece but to produce a better piece than they had before.

For that reason, teachers build opportunities for students to self-assess formatively into every writing sequence—as part of their overall intentional planning within the *Writing for Understanding* approach.

Formative Assessment, Feedback, and Revision at the Teacher Level

Revision in response to formative assessment happens at the teacher level as well as the individual student level. In a very real sense, *a teacher who is engaging with her students' writing, both within the student planning stage, during the actual composing process, after a "chunk," of writing, or after a whole first draft, is formatively assessing her own work with an eye to revising it.*

What does this mean? Simply this: a teacher's goal, in a *Writing for Understanding* sequence, is that his students show clear understanding in an appropriately well-crafted piece of writing. Keeping in mind who his students are, how old they are, what their strengths and needs are, and what he wants them to understand, he has developed a sequence of instruction that he hopes will bring them along further than they were.

Their writing is the result of his work. As he walks around the room while his students are writing, as he answers their questions or encourages them to answer them for themselves, he is asking himself similar questions to those that Sally and Julia asked. *Did my plan work? Are my students able to use the instruction I gave them? Do they show that they understand what they're doing?* As the teacher is assessing his students' first draft writing or working with them as they actually compose, he is doing more than giving feedback to individual students. He is also noticing patterns. If he notices, for example, that a great number of his third graders are good at sticking to a focus but are leaving out transitions, he can revise his teaching to emphasize that skill—on the spot, or in the next lesson. If he notices that many of them are confused about the ways that the Abenaki used plants, he knows that in some way he has given insufficient attention to that instruction and can revise his teaching to help his students.

In short, as he is using ongoing formative assessment to help individual students revise to clarify and develop their writing, the teacher himself is using ongoing formative assessment to revise his own instruction. What worked? What do students still need? What shall I do? It is all a part of *Writing for Understanding* planning.

Inside the Classroom: Four Teachers Plan for Drafting and Revision

Planning for drafting and revision can take a great variety of forms in the *Writing for Understanding* classroom. Here, four teachers show different approaches, each reflecting the teacher's purpose with his or her own instructional plan.

Revision at the Planning Stage: Upper Elementary Informational Writing

A fifth-grade class was busy with research on famous artists. It was the spring of the school year, and students had done much work over the course of the year working with focused writing in a well-organized plan, using accurate supporting details (a modified Painted Essay format). The teacher believed that, after reading and note-taking on an artist, her students were ready to choose a focus for themselves, then develop a plan for their writing and go ahead and write.

One student, Carlotta, decided to work with one of the three focusing questions that her teacher had posed: "What personal qualities of the artist helped him/her become famous?" Below is her plan for her work on artist Georgia O'Keefe.

Thesis:

Georgia O'Keefe's qualities are determination and creativity.

Determination:

• became an artist

• not stop painting

• to be creative

Creativity:

• big paintings

• a lot of money

• look like photos

Using this plan, Carlotta went ahead and wrote her first draft.

Life with Georgia O'Keefe
By Carlotta

Swerve like a paintbrush into this article and find out about Georgia O'Keefe's past as an artist.

Qualities

That's one of Georgia O'Keefe's paintings. (Poppy picture next to this paragraph.) She is one of the most important artists recognized in America back in 1986.

Georgia O'Keefe has a lot of determination, creativity, and symbolism. She's a very talented artist.

Determination

"I'm going to be one of the most famous painters in America," claimed Georgia O'Keefe. Georgia O'Keefe was determined to become an artist at the age of 12. For example when she started her career as a painter she was determined to not stop even if people said they didn't like her paintings. She was also determined to be creative with her paintings like this one. (Sky Above the Clouds painting next to this paragraph.) She was determined to keep on painting because when her eye-sight began to fail in 1971. She started to sculpt clay. In the way she did her paintings.

Symbolizing

Georgia O'Keefe uses a lot of symbolism. Her flowers are symbolic to a new life blooming into the world. Also when she lost her eyesight she had to sculpt clay. She sculpted it with all the curves symbolizing her paintings. Her sculptures had the same feeling size and motions as her paintings. It took a lot of talent to be able to sculpt when she was blind.

Creativity

Creativity is one of Georgia O'Keefe's qualities. She was creative in many ways. For instance when she was so creative when people bought her paintings they spent a lot of money on just on of her paintings. She used bright colors and that's what people recognized her from. She also did big paintings so people saw them the way she saw them. Because she was so creative she was offered to model her paintings for Alfred Stielglitz. After a while the fell in love and got married. She was creative with many of her paintings.

Style

Georgia O'Keefe was very well known for her style. Like when she painted nature. Because nature inspired her from when she was just a baby. She remembered the blanket that she was placed upon. She remembered all the patterns and designs. That were on the blanket. She used bright colors so people would recognize that that is her art. By just looking at the painting. They would recognize the bright colors, sculls and the flowers. She painted by zooming in on the object even if it were as small as an ant.

Unique Georgia

She was a talented artist. Her style, determination, creativity and symbolism were Georgia O'Keefe's qualities. She used them in her paintings and in her life as a painter. Georgia O'Keefe was successful with her paintings because of her qualities. You can tell she put a lot of work into all of her paintings. And she took her time. Because she was a unique women. Her art will be recognized throughout the century.

When Carlotta's teacher read this piece, she realized that Carlotta did have a solid sense of structure. She knew how to organize informational writing, and she had done so independently.

She also recognized, however, that Carlotta did not have a clear understanding of what she was doing in some ways. Once again, let's listen in on the conversation the teacher had with herself as she read this draft.

"Hmmm. This student is confused, especially about what 'creativity' means. Her paragraph on creativity does not really make sense. Besides that, I can see that she has added paragraphs on 'symbolism' and 'style' that were not in her original plan, and she has included them as if they were separate qualities instead of being an aspect of creativity.

"Let me look back at the plan she wrote before going ahead with this draft. Well, right there I can see a problem. She seems to think that 'creativity' has something to do with making money, and she doesn't seem to understand that style and symbolism are really a part of O'Keefe's creativity. That misunderstanding seems pretty clear right in the plan she wrote before the draft.

"Let's see—how many other students seem to have had this problem, of really not completely understanding their own plans before they began writing? Not many, but definitely some. Carlotta is not the only one.

"Okay, I can see how I need to revise this instructional process for next time. I need to have each student explain her plan out loud to me before going ahead with writing. If I had asked Carlotta to explain her plan to me orally, before writing, I would have caught Carlotta's misunderstanding much earlier, before she had done all that writing. That's a good lesson for me, I guess!"

The teacher here is recognizing an important opportunity for students to revise their work—during the planning stage of a piece of writing, before drafting. She could see that working clearly with the ideas of the piece was something she could not always assume a student could do, even when the student had the structural idea of what the plan should look like.

The teacher also has clearly and effectively revised her own instruction. Next time, she will make sure to pay attention to what students are writing as they plan, and make sure she heads off misunderstanding at the pass!

Revising during Writing: Upper Elementary Narrative Writing

Here, a fourth-grade class is just beginning to work on narrative writing. In this case, students already have a good grasp of the elements fundamental to writing any narrative—the characters, the setting, the character motivation, the problem/conflict, and the resolution—from earlier intentional instruction. Now, the teacher has given specific instruction in creating leads. Each student has a photograph and a plan for using it to come up with the focus for a narrative; each student also already has a basic plan (in terms of the narrative elements) for that story.

This student is writing in class, as are her fourth-grade classmates. Like them, she is working with ideas as she goes. She tries out some leads, reads them back, crosses them out, starts again (see following page).

What kind of planning did the teacher do for this revise-as-you-go form of drafting and revision? A look inside the teacher's head will clarify her planning process, a highly intentional but flexible process that would allow both her students and herself to formatively assess their work against a plan, get feedback, and revise as needed.

"So, I know everyone has a plan for a narrative that includes all the narrative elements (that was, after all, the central idea I had planned for!). We've listened to students describe these to each

Aby J.....

Here at the Blue Water ~~Greens~~ stand one young zebra ~~desperately~~ searching for food When the ~~zebra~~

~~Here at the Blue Water Greens~~ standed a young zebra

Bom Bom Its hunting time at The Blue Water Greens and all the ~~animals desperately~~ trying to get out of Kenya. ~~One~~ there was a zebra named Marcie. Marcie was ~~x~~ nice, smart, jerus and very creative. Marcie would say stuff but non of the animals would lisen to her. Some animals, would say that she was to creative and she had no feeling of the real world. She wanted people to lisen to her but with her weard imagonation. her voice was lost in the air.

Bom Bom by now every one is stilland silent all you could hear is the loud gun shuding. Macie has an I dia. She dashed across Blue Water Greens and told every one her plan. ~~They said no no that is a bad plan becaus when the~~

other. They seem pretty invested in the stories they're going to write. I'm glad I was able to get such good photographs for them —old calendars and magazines can be a real gold mine!

"They also have plenty of models of how narratives begin, and I'll make sure I keep all of those books available on the corner table so that they can reread them, it they like. I have at least a few kids who may be pretty dependent on those for ideas.

"It'll be pretty easy for me to make myself available while they write. I think I'll just weave around the room, just like I do when they're working on math problems—that way if anyone has a question or is stuck in some way, I'm right there to help.

"Also, I think it'll be important for me to encourage kids to read aloud frequently, so they can get help from each other, and everyone can be part of that conversation—that is *so* helpful for all of my students, especially the ones who struggle with language.

"I think this revise-as-you-draft technique is going to be a good way for my kids to really think about what they're doing, to check against what they're trying to say, and find ways to say it better—or maybe even change their mind about what they're trying to do, as they hear from other students.

"Now, I know from past experience that I may well have areas of confusion that are common to lots of kids—probably from areas I didn't give quite enough time to with instruction. With this approach, I'll be able to stop the class in midstream (or mid-sentence!) if I need to for a bit of a refresher about something. I'll be sure to build in some time to work around any surprises, rather than plan every minute of our class time. That way, I'll be able to address issues as they come up, though I might decide to deal with some of them in a later unit."

This teacher's instructional plan aims to help students produce thoughtful, effective narratives, including drafting and revision.

This plan reflects her knowledge of both the writing process and her own students.

This teacher's plan for drafting and revision—part of her overall instructional plan—reflects her knowledge of the elements that must be in place if students are to produce thoughtful, effective narratives as well as her understanding of the needs and abilities of her own students. She has recognized that students need both specific instruction before they write and a system of supported informal assessment and revision. They need both of these for this particular writing task, specifically, as well as for the development of transferable approaches to writing in general. Her planning allowed the student writer to approach writing thoughtfully and confidently, to formatively assess his own work, and to continue until he got something workable—not perfect, but workable. It also allowed the teacher to formatively assess her own instruction and step in where she could see she needed to, an approach from which everyone benefited.

Revision for Knowledge and Understanding during Writing: Middle School Persuasive Writing

Jennifer was a seventh-grade student whose class was studying a unit on global warming, a unit whose central idea was, "It will take many actions at many levels to manage global warming." At the end of the unit, each student was asked to choose one action that could help manage global warming (the focus), and write a persuasive op-ed letter for a newspaper.

Jennifer chose to write about the value of buying food locally. She wrote in class, self-assessing formatively and revising as she went. Excerpts of her persuasive letter appear below. The revisions appear in bold.

In this day and age, global warming isn't a brand new or mysterious phrase. But what does it really mean? And more importantly, what can we do to turn it around?

Global warming is happening because of human activity. Everyday things like driving cars, using computers and TV's, and taking showers all put CO_2 into the air. A regular amount of CO_2 traps solar rays into the atmosphere, and this keeps our planet at a nice, livable temperature, like a room temperature. But the abnormal amount of CO_2 in the atmosphere has changed the temperature of our planet drastically. And with the rising temperature comes huge glaciers melting to slivers of snow, higher numbers of severe droughts and hurricanes and animals being forced out of their natural habitats. The whole balance of nature is off.

And what can we do to balance the scales? There are many different paths to take. But one way will not solve global warming. This is a complex problem that takes complex solutions.

One possible solution is buying locally grown and organically grown foods. It is a fact that most American meals travel 1,500 miles from the farm to the plate....But if we buy our food from farmer's markets close by or at stores that carry local foods, the distance traveled to get this food from the farm to the plate is cut down, and therefore the amount of gas that is used is cut down. And in turn, that cuts down on CO_2 emissions. If every US citizen were to eat just one meal a week of locally and organically grown foods, then we would reduce the country's oil consumption by 1.1 million barrels—every week......

(several more supporting arguments appear here, before Jennifer proceeds to the counter argument)

It is very true that locally produced food is more expensive. Locally grown foods are a considerable amount more expensive than non-local foods, and this makes them **not accessible to those living on rigid budgets, like public schools or low-income (people). This all comes down to poor subsidizing. Right now, the government is subsidizing gas and oil, exactly what it takes to produce most food in stores today. So, things that don't take gas to be made aren't as cheap as oil-made food. This can be changed, however. Those who are concerned about where government dollars are being spent can push for adequate subsidies to be made for local local, organic food, to make them accessible for all.** Vote for presidential candidates who address this issue, or write to your legislator.

(Jennifer goes on with another support paragraph, then ends with this conclusion)

We have created a dilemma for ourselves. Global warming is a problem that will get the best of us—or our children—if we don't move and try to do something about it today. Solving global warming is like a puzzle. Every solution is just another piece, they fit together to create that last image, a global warming free future. Buying locally grown and produced food is a puzzle piece. It is a small part that can do a lot, if it is given the attention it deserves.

Jennifer has written thoughtfully and effectively (though, again, not perfectly) to persuade readers to support local food production as a way of managing global warming. Working within an overall plan of content, focus, and structure, she formatively assessed her writing against her own argument—that supporting local food production could help in the fight to manage global warming.

In this case, Jennifer was not concerned about the writing skills per se, but about her understanding of the ideas with which she was working. For her, revision was not about the crafting of the sentences or the use of words; rather, it was about the ideas—the knowledge and the understanding—themselves. As Jennifer formatively assessed her own thinking ("Does this make sense to me? Do I understand these ideas well enough to explain them?"), she discovered that she needed some help with making sense of those ideas. She realized that she wasn't quite clear on the details and needed to make sense of the complicated relationships between food, transportation, and government subsidies. After a short conversation with the teacher (and the school cook!), Jennifer had clarified her thinking orally so that she was able to work with those ideas in her piece.

What did the teacher's plan look like to get the student to this point? How did she plan for revision so that Jennifer and the other students in the class were able to revise as they drafted? Once more, we'll look at the teacher's thinking as she developed her approach both to giving students the opportunity to formatively assess their work and to checking in on her own instruction to see what had worked and what needed revising.

"Well, I hope I have the energy for this—we've been working on this global warming unit, and now everybody has chosen something from his or her own area of interest to write about as part of the solution to managing global warming. So there's some real release of responsibility to students here. Yikes! I hope we're all ready for this!

"I know that the first line of defense will be to have a short conference or conversation with each kid—*each* kid—before he or she writes. With all these different focuses (okay, foci), I'll be asking for trouble if I don't do that. I can have those conversations while they're working on vocab homework. Since they don't need my attention for the homework, I won't have to run around to keep people on task.

"I'm sure I'll catch some of the problems right there, at that planning stage, but I also know I won't catch everything. This is tough stuff, tough content…I want to make sure they have their unit notes easily available and that I'm available, too, to help kids get a better handle on their ideas or even to locate specific facts or statistics. They may well need to go back for more information, to develop a greater understanding. I'll be sure to plan so that everyone has time to gather any additional information.

"It's funny—I have a feeling that even my ordinarily strong writers are going to need to do some deeper work with their ideas once they get past their plan and start writing—I'm guessing that they'll realize they just don't know enough yet, in some cases, about their own argument—well, that's what revising ideas is all about! I'll also need to check in with each student during the drafting stage, to make sure that the ideas that seemed clear when they were planning are still clear now that it's time to put them into sentences. If I find any students who are having trouble clarifying ideas, I can help them identify the source of their problem, then help them figure out how to solve it—again, sometimes by going back for more information.

"This whole writing phase will also give me a chance to see how well my own instruction has paid off. I know I have a big range of ages and experience in this class, and this piece is going to need a somewhat different introduction than they're used to. Well, I might need to pull a small group aside to work on that. Oh, and they're working with citations for only the second time—I wonder if I spent enough time on that? I guess I'll see!"

Revision after a First Draft: Upper Elementary Informational Writing

Early in the fall of fourth grade, a class was working with informational writing. The teacher had given the students the focusing question, "What place is important to you?" and had asked them to write independently. In this particular case, the teacher had two goals. One was to get a baseline on her incoming students, to see where they were on an independent level in terms of the elements of writing: how well could they focus, plan, organize, and support their ideas? The second was to begin to give students an opportunity for self-assessment and revision. In this assignment, the teacher chose a generic question, much like a state assessment would, so that each student would have adequate information easily at hand and could concentrate on using the elements of writing (focus, organization, detail, voice/tone) appropriately.

Here is the independent work of one struggling student, Philip (who, a year earlier, cried when he needed to write at all).

Every year me, my brothers Levi and Kris, and my dad go to Old Orchard Beach in Maine. Last summer we went. It took us five hours to get there. Old Orchard is my favorite place because of the food and the beach.

The food in Maine is delicious. One time I was there and all I ate for two days was pizza! my dad bought fried dough and the seagulls stole it. Also, the fries in Maine are the best fries I have ever tasted. Man, the food in Maine is great.

Once you have your food, you can eat it on the beach. Just look out for the seagulls! The beach is great because of the swimming, but the water is very cold. I also like to boogie board because all the waves are very big. When I lose the feeling in my legs, I go and make a sand castle.

Man, the food and the beach are great! I go there every year. So next time you are in Maine, GO!!! to Old Orchard Beach.

Below is Philip's revised essay. Notice that he has not added many details, but those that he has added have clearly enhanced his meaning. He has made his writing more effective.

Every year me, my brothers Levi and Kris, and my dad go to Old Orchard Beach in Maine. Last summer we went. It took us five hours to get there. **We left at 1:00 in the morning.** Old Orchard is my favorite place because of the food and the beach.

The food in Maine is delicious. One time I was there and all I ate for two days was pizza! **One of the pizzas had very spicy sausage. Another time** my dad bought fried dough and the seagulls stole it. **Those evil seagulls!** Also, the fries in Maine are the best fries I have ever tasted. Man, the food in Maine is great.

Once you have your food, you can eat it on the **great** beach. Just look out for the seagulls! The beach is great because of the swimming, but the water is *very* cold. I also like to boogie board because all the waves are very big. **One time a wave made my boogie board hit me in the stomach.** When I lose the feeling in my legs, I go and make a sand castle.

> Man, the food and the beach are great! I go there
> every year. So next time you are in Maine, GO!!! to
> Old Orchard Beach.

How did the teacher plan for this type of after-the-first-draft formative assessment and revision? Again, we'll take a look at the conversation she had with herself as she planned.

"Okay, I'm hoping to get some good information from this prompt about which skills my students have and which they don't have (which partly means what was taught well and what teachers didn't pay enough attention to, and of course a whole host of other things—writing is complicated!)

"So, first I'll notice what they did well, what seems to be working, what they've internalized. Then I'll keep track of what isn't working well enough yet, what their needs are. Of course, not everyone's needs will be the same, so some needs will be individual—but I bet I'll also see some patterns. And, after all, I do need that information—it's how I decide what I need to emphasize from here on, in my teaching.

"But I also want to see how effectively my kids are self-assessing and give them an opportunity to do more of it. I don't want to tell them 'change this' or 'change that.' Really, what I need to do is give them an opportunity to think about what they're trying to say, what meaning they're creating, what they want their reader to understand (since that *is* what writing is all about!).

"So, after their first drafts are complete, I think if I give manageable feedback—say, two or three observations—it'll give each student a chance to think about his intention for this writing, then do a bit of revising to make the piece more effective.

"For this particular student, I want to make that feedback pretty concrete—I know what a struggling writer he is and how easily he shuts down. Maybe if I say, 'tell us more about what that seagull was like,' and 'give us readers a sense of how big those waves really were,' that will give him an idea of how to elaborate a bit."

This teacher had a clear sense of what it took for young writers, including struggling writers, to internalize what it takes to write clearly. She knew about how much students can handle effectively in revision, and she knew that students, especially struggling students, need guided feedback. Vygotsky's "zone of proximal development" was a place this teacher spent a lot of time with her students.

Further, the teacher herself had a forward-looking plan. She knew that her fourth graders would spend a lot of time over the course of the year with developing more accuracy, precision, and clarity in writing. With all of this in mind, she planned for appropriate feedback to the student (she did *not* write for him) that he was free to use as he revised. Clearly, this struggling student did just that.

In all of these examples, teachers included planning for assessment, feedback, and revision as a connected and integral part of an overall plan to help students construct meaning effectively in writing, and to help themselves teach more effectively. In each case, students were able to succeed as a result of that teacher planning. Their writing is not perfect—nobody would mistake it for professional work. More importantly, though, than achieving perfection, each student was able to build meaning. Each student was able to approach a thinking/writing task, stand back from it to formatively assess if it was working, and make changes so that the work made sense. In the end, each was able to stand back from a finished piece of work with a sense of competence and confidence and say, "Hey, I get this!" Each teacher was also able to formatively assess her own instruction and build that assessment into her overall instruction and support for the students, so that their sense of confidence and real competence could continue to grow.

In *Writing for Understanding*, all of this teacher planning has "transfer" as its ultimate goal. Ultimately, we want all our students, all along the way, to experience meaning-making in all of their writing and to develop the writing skills that will make them increasingly able to do that. We want them to experience, over and over again, what it feels like to understand and to make sense in effective writing. And we want them to become increasingly independent in all aspects of their writing. In the next chapter, we will take a look at what that transfer can look like in writing, and what students say about it.

TO SUMMARIZE....

- **Planning for drafting includes planning for revision, and drafting itself involves revision.**

- **It is helpful to think of revision as a form of formative assessment for both student and teacher. A student who is revising his writing is "checking it" against his plan for constructing meaning and getting feedback on how to make that meaning more clear. A teacher who is helping students revise is also formatively assessing her own instruction ("What did they get? What did they not get? What do I need to do next time?").**

- **Revision can—and should—happen at any or all stages of writing—at the planning stage, while writing, after a completed draft.**

Section III
Transfer to Independence

Chapter Six:
Transfer in Writing

Christopher Robin is going.
At least I think he is.
Where?
Nobody knows.
But he is going—
I mean he goes
(To rhyme with "knows")
Do we care?
(To rhyme with "where")
We do
Very much.
(I haven't got a rhyme for that
"is" in the second line yet.
Bother.)
(Now I haven't got a rhyme for bother.
Bother.)
Those two bothers will have to rhyme with each other Buther.

The fact is, this is more difficult
than I thought,
I ought—
(Very good indeed)
I ought
To begin again,
But it is easier
To stop.
Christopher Robin, good-bye,
I
(Good)
I
And all your friends
Sends—
I mean all your friend
Send—
(Very awkward this, it keeps going wrong)
Well, anyhow, we send
Our love.
END.

—*A.A. Milne,* The House at Pooh Corner

Eeyore the donkey has been given an important charge. It is near the end of the book, and Christopher Robin is about to undergo a momentous change: he is going off to school. The creatures in the Hundred Acre Wood are giving him a party, and Eeyore has been chosen to write the speech.

Eeyore has never been in this situation before. He has never had to compose a poem, and Christopher Robin has never gone off to school. But Eeyore knows how to approach the task. He knows what he wants to say—his focus, his central idea. He has an overall plan for what he wants to say to Christopher Robin, and he hopes to say it well—even, perhaps, movingly. Further, he knows that all the other creatures will be there, listening. In short, Eeyore takes his responsibility seriously.

So he begins to write. Like many writing tasks, this one turns out to be a bit harder than Eeyore had anticipated, but he is undaunted. As he chooses the actual words and crafts the sentences, Eeyore listens to his own voice and his own language and finds that he needs to tweak. He needs to rearrange some words and deal with some troublesome rhymes. Very aware of his focus within his overall central idea, he keeps checking back in with it to make sure he is saying what he wants to say.

And in the end, even though the writing is not perfect, Eeyore writes successfully: his meaning is clear, to himself and to his audience.

Eeyore has accomplished what we hope for all of our students, no matter their grade level. Faced with a meaningful, real-life challenge that requires writing, he has successfully transferred his learning about writing to this new situation. His work is not perfect, but it is effective and successful. As A.A. Milne informs us, "They all clapped."

What is Transfer?

According to the National Research Council, whose book *How People Learn* (2000) has provided a rich explanation of what science knows so far about learning, transfer is "the ability to extend what has been learned in one context to new contexts."

If we think about it, transfer is really the reason we send people to school. We teach children to read so that they will be able to pick up a *Curious George* book or *To Kill A Mockingbird* or the newspaper or material from an Internet site on the latest research on diabetes and read it thoughtfully, for joy or meaning or both. We teach people to use mathematics so they can count their crayons or figure out their credit card interest rate or decide whether those statistics about Social Security could possibly be accurate or figure out whether that rent is too high. We teach people to write so that they can make a card for Grandma or keep a personal journal or analyze a State of the Union speech or write up their research or deliver a tribute at a friend's wedding.

In short, we teach for transfer. We teach so that students are able to use the knowledge they have and the habits of mind that they have acquired to make sense of and navigate in the world as they encounter it, all along the way.

Transfer is not an "all-or-nothing" skill. It is not black and white. It is not something one either can or cannot do. Transfer of any skill or knowledge or habit of mind is not tested in a "one-shot" way and then put away, stamped "done: transfer completed." Rather, it is best viewed as a dynamic process in which one is engaging constantly, at various levels, sometimes even with various amounts of assistance, depending on the situation (National Research Council 2000).

Eeyore did not write his speech during language arts period. No one told him what his focus should be, and no one reminded him to include details. Eeyore was on his own, and he was able to transfer what he had already learned about writing to this new task. In the end, he did not produce a "perfect piece" (his creator, A. A. Milne, could undoubtedly have written a more sophisticated piece!). But he was able to call on what he knew, both about his central idea and about writing craft, remind himself of it frequently, and come up with a coherent piece of meaningful writing.

It worked. Everybody clapped.

What do We Mean by "Transfer" When It Comes to Writing?

Writing is all about understanding. As we know, the *Writing for Understanding* instructional approach is premised on the idea that to write effectively and successfully, students need:

- a solid knowledge base for their ideas—one cannot write about what one does not know or understand at an appropriate level;

- a focus through which to think about and frame that knowledge, to drive the plan for writing;

- a clear grasp of appropriate tools—a structure to guide the writer's thinking and make it clear to the reader, plus whatever craft techniques can appropriately enliven, clarify, and deepen the meaning of the writing

- an expectation of sense-making, the habit of mind of knowing what "making sense" feels like (as opposed to confusion or a vague or fuzzy grasp of the content) in writing

As they learn, student writers develop their skills through instruction that the teacher has planned carefully and feedback that she has given. As time progresses, though, the teacher slowly removes the scaffolding, asking students to become more independent in remembering what is required and putting it into action. She helps them to become increasingly able to transfer their knowledge to a context or problem that is new to them, as Eeyore did.

In his moving speech, Eeyore succeeded in transfer. He showed knowledge of his subject, knowledge that grew from his longtime relationship with Christopher Robin. He worked to focus his speech on the love that he wanted to send to his friend. He used appropriate tools, considering structure and rhyme. And throughout, he expected to make and communicate sense. Eeyore persisted doggedly, checking up on his work frequently, until his poem gets across the desired message.

What Does It Take for Students to Transfer? What Makes Transfer Possible?

The National Research Council's *How People Learn* has pulled together the existing research on what elements need to be in place if children are (in fact, if anyone is) going to successfully transfer understanding and skills to a situation that is in some way new and untried—maybe partially, maybe completely. While the authors acknowledge that there is still much we do not know about learning and transfer, they nevertheless point out that we know a good deal which, if we could put it into the hands of teachers, would make a difference in how successful education is.

These elements include:

Adequate initial learning.   Students need to have worked with ideas deeply and frequently before they own them sufficiently to transfer those ideas to a new situation. This idea seems so obvious that it does not even warrant repeating, but the authors point out that it is common *not* to give students enough practice or experience with whatever knowledge they will be expected to transfer—and that therefore, transfer cannot occur. An idea that flits across a student's radar screen, that gets ten minutes of a mini-lesson, is not an idea for which a student has had adequate "initial learning."

The ability to abstract understanding of underlying concepts.   Students who can understand abstractions—central principles which can be applied flexibly to various situations and contexts—are far more likely to be able to transfer learning to new contexts or tasks. Again, according to the National Research Council, "research studies generally provide strong support for the benefits of helping students represent their experiences at levels of abstraction that transcend the specificity of particular contexts and examples" (National Research Council 1994, p. 65).

The catch here is that *abstraction will not occur if students do not have enough opportunity—a lot of opportunity—to work with specific knowledge, in specific contexts.* We human beings do not seem able to grasp a flexible abstraction of an idea unless it emerges through a kind of synthesizing process, drawn from many specific contexts. Research indicates that when these specific contexts are numerous and varied, then the ability to develop deep understanding, then flexibly transfer it, is much more likely to develop.

Time to learn.   This "time to learn" is clearly closely related to initial learning. Students need to spend significant time with the ideas that they will be expected to transfer. According to the authors, the pattern recognition, the connections between ideas that allow students to build "chunks" of meaning out of many specific facts and ideas, and that allow them to abstract, can come only from having worked with information and ideas for a significant amount of time.

Self-monitoring and using feedback as an ingrained habit of mind.   When students have the frequent experience of self-monitoring, of checking in on themselves and their thinking (as Eeyore did), research shows that they are far more likely to be able to transfer those ideas and knowledge and skills to a new task.

Motivation to learn.   People are born problem solvers. According to the National Research Council, "we have a need to solve problems" (p. 102). If students have had frequent and successful experiences in meeting challenges that are appropriately difficult (not too easy, which is boring, or too hard, which is frustrating), they are likely to be motivated to persevere at a transfer task until they meet the challenge.

Writing for Understanding Supports Transfer

The principles and approaches that make up *Writing for Understanding* instruction reflect these understandings about transfer.

First, a *Writing for Understanding* sequence of instruction is based on making sure students have a solid grasp of what they will be writing about. This is why teacher planning for student content mastery is so central to what students will ultimately experience. The teacher in the *Writing for Understanding* classroom knows the central idea he wants students to understand and to demonstrate in writing. He knows what focusing question he will pose to students to frame their thinking. He plans for solid acquisition of that knowledge on the part of the students, with many opportunities along the way for both the students and the teacher to make sure they understand the information they are gathering—the words, the ideas, the relationships.

Further, the teacher in the *Writing for Understanding* classroom recognizes that a successful, effective piece of writing is a meeting of clear understanding and a logical, meaning-making structure. He does not leave this to chance. Instead, he incorporates into his planning scaffolding in structure appropriate to the grade level, experience, and skills of his students.

After that, he incorporates instruction in specific elements of writer's craft that will help his students write as thoughtfully and effectively as possible. This instruction might focus on types of leads; it might emphasize giving examples; it might involve working with dependent clauses; it might include instruction in citations or the use of counterarguments. Whatever it is, he makes sure students have adequate knowledge of it *before they begin to write.*

Finally, the teacher in the *Writing for Understanding* classroom builds in time and opportunity for self-monitoring and feedback. In this way, the students are experiencing, in a supported setting, what it feels like to step back from their work and check in on their understanding and their meaning-making in writing. In the same vein, the teacher monitors himself and his instruction and makes changes when he sees students' needs.

The result for students of this kind of planning is successful and effective writing—that is, writing that makes sense to them, makes sense to other people, and gives the students a sense of clarity (in their writing) and competence (about themselves).

This experience happens over and over again in the *Writing for Understanding* classroom. Students write using different content (which they understand), in different genres (which are appropriately scaffolded), using different focusing concepts (thesis/support, cause/effect, etc.). In the process, from these multiple, varied, specific writing contexts and tasks, students begin to abstract. They begin to abstract general principles about understanding, so that they recognize when they understand what they are writing about and when they need more information or greater clarity. And they begin to abstract general principles about the relationship between coherence and structure, coming to understand that all writing has a focus, an organizational plan, and accurate, thoughtful support. Self-monitoring becomes, for these students, a habit of mind, a way of life when writing.

What Transfer in *Writing for Understanding* Can Look Like: Some Examples

Here, students who have had much instruction in *Writing for Understanding* are writing for a variety of purposes. In each case, the writing shows the students' ability to transfer what they know about writing to a new context or task.

Primary Response to Text. This piece was successfully written by a struggling second grader, Lucinda. Her teacher had read aloud, several times, the text that Lucinda is discussing, so Lucinda knew the text well before she began to write.

The Picteurs Say It All
By Lucinda

I read the book **Lilly's PuRPLe Plastic PuRse** and the book would be nothing without the pictures beceuse they are so powerful to the book. The pitures where teling the book and I Just Love the pictures so much. In the book Lilly got feres and mad at her teacher. The pictures show Lilly's eyes are big red and round and look like they popping out of her head. Just by looking at the pictures you can Just tel how mad she is. On anthe paJ LiLLY is skiping and hopping all the way home. She is smiling and leaping of the paj you can tell frme the pictures that she is very happy. The pictures in this book are amazing and help you out stand how Lilly fels.

What knowledge, understanding, and habits of mind has Lucinda transferred to be able to produce such an effective piece of writing? What instruction did her teacher plan and then carry out so that Lucinda and so many of her classmates were able to transfer that knowledge successfully?

In this case, working with young children with little writing experience, the teacher planned deliberately for transfer. Planning backwards in September, she decided that by the spring of that year, she wanted her students to be independently able to understand a picture book, responding to it in terms of the craft the author used to make the book effective. Depending on the text, their response might discuss language, pictures, or rhymes or patterns. Her goal for them was to be able to clearly construct meaning in writing, using the most basic structure of focus, supporting evidence from the text, and concluding statement. In other words, she planned for her students to be able to construct a solid paragraph, with all the detail of that paragraph coming from specific evidence from the text.

Knowing that this goal was fully aligned with Vermont state standards for independent writing and that she would be able to address the needs of a range of students in her class, the teacher planned a sequence of instruction that first gave students a great deal of experience with "oral paragraphs." She then wove in writing, using the same emphasis on using a focus and supporting evidence that she had done in the oral work, and building as she went. Over the course of the year, students had many opportunities to talk through and construct understanding in writing.

By the spring of the year, the teacher was ready to assess her students' ability to transfer their understanding to an independently written response to text. She gave her students a focusing question, asking them to explain what made the book so effective (author's craft), told them they needed to work on their own, and set them to work.

Lucinda was off and running. Her teacher was delighted to see that this struggling student was able to transfer her understanding independently with this task. She transferred her understanding of both the writer's craft (the content) and the elements of writing at a second-grade level, and so did many of her classmates. The teacher noticed that a few students were not able to transfer their understanding fully, but their struggles provided her with useful information, pushing her to think about how she might revise her own instruction the next year.

Upper elementary informational writing. The following two pieces were written by a fourth grader, Tom. He wrote the first one at the beginning of the year, after very direct, guided instruction about the Painted Essay in responding to text, and the other from an independent prompt at the end of the year. Tom is not a struggling student; however, his work shows what transfer can look like within the context of beginning to work with a Painted Essay structure.

Character Essay on Dewey
from Trouble River

Trouble River is a book about a pioneer boy named Dewey and his grandma. They are forced to escape down the river on Dewey's homemade raft when Indians attack. Dewey is the most interesting character in the book because he is brave, resourceful and determined.

First of all Dewey is brave. For example he tries to scare the Indian away from the cabin even if he might get hurt. Another time, Dewy shows he is brave when he takes his Grandma out on a raft he's never steered before down Trouble River where whole wagons have gone down in the quicksand!

Dewey is also resourceful. This can be seen when he earns money by picking up bones and selling them to buy nails for his raft. It is also apparent when he makes a raft out of logs and rawhide without any help from anyone.

Most importantly, Dewey is determined. He shows this when he is determined to get to the Dargan's and then to Hunter City, where he knows he and his grandma will be safe.

In conclusion, Dewey is the most interesting character in the book. He is brave, resourceful and determined. Trouble River is a book that is hard to put down. It is interesting, exciting and full of suspense. As a reader I could feel Dewey's determination to make it down Trouble River alive.

Tom's work on this essay was highly scaffolded, through an introduction to the Painted Essay. Tom painted the template in blue and yellow, mixed the colors together to make green, and structured his paragraphs to mirror the picture he had created. His class had collected public notes on the characteristics that Dewey, the main character, displayed, finding evidence in the book that supported their ideas. Tom wrote a successful essay, and he wrote the actual piece independently, but he had not yet been asked to transfer.

At the end of the year, after many opportunities to practice clear thinking and focused, well-structured writing—again, about text, about content, about experiences—Tom was given a transfer task. The assessment asked him simply to, "Write about someone you admire." Tom's task was to transfer all of his knowledge and understanding and respond independently to this prompt. "I know a lot about my dad," he said to himself, "I know what understanding feels like, and I know how to focus and organize to help me and my readers understand about why I admire my Dad—so I can make a plan."

My Dad

One person I really admire is my Dad. He is always helpful and always there when I need him. My Dad is fun, encouraging and helpful.

First of all my Dad is fun. He can make a dull day really exciting. He plays lots of jokes and games with me. He can also make chores fun by giving the first person done a dime. It seems like he can always think of something fun to do.

Also my Dad is encouraging. For example, he is really proud of me when I get a good report card. He also wants me to be really good at sports. Whenever I'm stuck he's always there to cheer me on. Whenever he cheers for me something inside just makes me do my best. I don't think I've ever done something good that he hasn't praised.

Most importantly my Dad is helpful. He's always there to coach me through the bad times. Like when I get a really tough homework assignment he's always there to give advice. Some with sports, or how much money I should spend at one time. My Dad is always there to help me, right when I need him.

In conclusion it seems like my Dad will do anything to help me or other people. He helps me do my best but he makes it fun too. My Dad is one person I really admire. And of course, he is my Dad!

Like Lucinda the second grader, Tom has successfully transferred his knowledge and understanding about building meaning in writing to this task, and it works. Nobody has said, "Tom, use the Painted Essay." Nobody has supplied him with graphic organizer of any sort.

Instead, he has internalized the ideas of order and coherence within a structure. Independently, Tom was able to focus his thinking, gather evidence of what he knows, and use a structure to make that thinking clear—to himself as the writer and to his readers.

Middle School Persuasive Writing

The following two pieces were written at the very end of the year, the first by a sixth grader, the second by an eighth grader. Over the course of the year (in fact, over the course of many years; these students have written a great deal in their school's writing program), the students had had many opportunities to share, discuss, and write about ideas in academic content areas. They were used to the idea of constructing meaning about specific content and expressing their ideas in focused, structured writing, using craft techniques both to expand and develop their thinking and to make their writing more engaging to an audience.

In this case, the sixth-, seventh-, and eighth-grade students had completed a very short study of the microloan system in Bangladesh that won the Nobel Prize in 2006 for Mohammed Yunus. Students had worked with economic concepts over the course of the year and then focused their study on Yunus and the Grameen Bank, the institution that made the microloans. Their teacher wanted to see how well they could show understanding of the importance of microcredit in getting people out of poverty (the central idea), and how well they could transfer their writing skills in this independent task.

In a culminating assessment, students were asked to respond to this prompt: "In the persona of a person who has benefited from a Grameen Bank microloan, write a letter to Mr. Yunus persuading him to continue those microloans to developing countries. Be sure you explain who you are and how you personally have benefited from the loan."

It is helpful to note that the teacher was looking for several different types of understanding in this task. She wanted to see if students could:

- transfer their understanding of the content itself (the impact of the Grameen Bank microloans) to a new situation;

- understand on a more empathetic level—to feel how individual lives are affected by poverty and then by hope;

- transfer their knowledge of the elements of effective writing—focus, structure, development, voice/tone—to this persuasive task.

The first piece is by a sixth-grade student, Melissa, who has worked hard to write effectively.

Dear Mr. Yunus,

My name is Urian, I live in Brazil. I have a husband and two children, (and) we were very poor. I got my loan a few weeks ago. I used to buy a shop next door to my home where my husband and I sell pottery now. Before I learned about the Grameen loan I had to sell pottery on the streets, and no one would buy my pottery. They give me respect now that I have money.

I had no clean water for my family, but now that I have the loan, I got cleaner water for my family. I also got a better education for my two children. One more way your loans have helped change the way my family and I live it it gave us more tools to make better selling pottery.

The loan helped to change my life in many ways. It taught me to be responsible for what I owned; it also taught me to be respectful and pay back the loan I took. I learned that more people treat you the way they should when you have the money and your family gets everything they need to help them get through tough times. This idea changed me to understand that people should always care about life and how one person helping thousands can change everything that happens. I thought it would be hard to pay back the loan, but when we opened up our shop, we made enough money to pay back the loan. I feel like I have done what is right for my family, and that is all that matters to me now.

Mr. Yunus, I know that it is hard to do all that you do for these villages in these countries, but even though many people have already gotten these loans, you should not give up on the people who have not gotten their loans yet. I know that it was very hard for my family to decide whether or not to use your program. Now I am glad we decided to, so please do not take this opportunity away from other people who are not sure to take a chance to help their family in many ways, like I have helped mine. I know that you can help stop poverty if you keep the Grameen loan going.

Thank you.

The next piece is by a seventh-grade writer, Ricardo.

Dear Mr. Yunis,

My name is Jose Costello. I am a hat maker, but I wouldn't be if it weren't for you and Grameen loans. In fact, I would be living on the streets of Puerto Rico. I escaped from Cuba at age 12 with my father who was killed on the journey to Puerto Rico, my mother got sick and died when I was three. So when I arrived here I was alone and hungry, and it was not until I make it to Jamaica where my grandparents live did I get any real food.

The next time you were in our village, I showed up at one of your meetings and luckily you allowed me to get a loan. The next day I took the money and bought the materials I needed to start up my hat business. With the money I had left, I fixed up the small excuse of a house that we lived in. My business started out slow, but soon enough I had what I needed to pay back the loan and then some. After I paid you back, I kept up my business until I was at the point where I lived in a three room house, every night I had a full meal, and never again did I have to drink water that wasn't clean.

The real reason I am writing is because, one, I wanted to thank you, and two, I wanted you to know that you really shouldn't stop giving out Grameen loans. If you did, so many people would be left in the poverty they are in now. For instance a friend of mine and her son live on the street with no water, no food, and no shelter. If she were to get one of your loans she could start a business and eventually be able to send her son to school and she could get shelter and food and water.

Mr. Yunis you pulled me out of the dirt that is poverty and cleaned me off, and now I am the happiest man I have ever been and I have never felt so self-sufficient. You are obviously a kind, generous man; I know this because even though I am not a woman like I am supposed to be in order to get a loan (note; 97% of Grameen loans go to women) you still allowed my to get one. So if you are so kind, then you should be able to see that if you keep up Grameen loans then soon enough you will have freed everyone from poverty's chain-like death grip.

Sincerely,

Your friend Jose Costello

What have these students transferred? In this case, the transfer is more general, more global. Their teacher wanted to see how well students could take a small body of content knowledge and apply that knowledge, empathetically and engagingly, to show understanding in a persuasive writing task. They needed to transfer their experience and expectation of meaning-making, their knowledge of a new set of information, and their abstracted understanding of the elements of writing, to a new context, and come up with a plan that worked. Like virtually all (though not quite all) of their classmates, both Melissa and Ricardo were successful with that transfer.

"Real World" Transfer

Transfer does not occur only in an academic context. When students truly internalize a skill and a habit of thought, it is theirs—available to use for a variety of reasons, in a variety of contexts.

The first piece was written as a thank you note by a sixth grader. Again, this student has used what she knows about clear thinking and effective writing: focus, structure, supporting details specific to that purpose (which in this case includes audience, the writer's older cousin who has given her make-up for her birthday!).

Dear Susie,

Thank you so much for the make-up, I love it! I have my beauty routine all planned out!

1. First, I wash my face.
2. I then put the sunscreen on.
3. Then comes the moisturizer.
4. My favorite, the blushing gel.
5. To lessen the effect, I sweep translucent powder over the gel.
6. For extra color I put some regular blush on.
7. I dab some concealer on either side of my eyes.
8. So it well stay on, brush translusent powder over the concealer.
9. To minimize shine I then powder my face with translusent powder.

By this time mom is on her way upstairs to tell me she can't give me a ride and if I don't come down this instant and eat my breakfast that she'll make me come down!

I'm having my birthday party today and we'll probably experiment with it! I'm really excited, thanks so much!

Love, Marian

Like Lucinda and Tom, Melissa and Ricardo, Marian needed to transfer what she knew about making sense in writing to this new context. Knowing her subject well (very well!), she was able to focus her thinking around thanking her cousin, then support it clearly and specifically. Marian has almost certainly written other thank you notes, so she has internalized a basic structure. Further, she has the habit of addressing her audience in a very targeted way, and using specific details that will connect her and her cousin (part of the implicit purpose of a thank-you letter). But nothing in this thank-you note suggests rote learning. Marian is not a slave to a rigid structure that she learned in class. Because she had internalized the central idea that writing is about meaning, Marian, without a given formula, without teacher direction, had made a plan in her head for her writing, and her transfer is effective and successful.

The next piece below is a nomination written, independently at home, by a seventh grader. Alicia used the skills taught in writing class to nominate a friend for a sportsmanship award established in honor of a former classmate.

I think Kristen deserves this sportsmanship award because of her outgoing optimism at all times, on and off the field. During basketball I was new and thought I made a ton of mistakes (I did). Kristen convinced me that she had made so many more mistakes and that it did not matter. When we were playing wiffle ball in P.E., someone said that they could not, for the life of them, hit a wiffle ball. Kristen said with sarcasm, but jokingly, "Oh that's positive!" and when they said that they were superb (at wiffle ball), Kristen said she agreed—they were correct. Kristen is always full of enthusiasm.

During our first tournament against Thetford, we were all nervous. She led us in a cheer that involved standing in a huddle and jumping around screaming. Through all of her energy, Kristen is still very sensitive. Before my very first basketball game, I was nervous. She was really hyped to go, but she took a minute and reassured me. She told me it wouldn't matter what happened, it was only a game. Because of Kristen's love for sports, love for people and general love for the world, I think Kristen is the perfect example of the sportsmanship Marshall would have wanted to see.

In this nomination, Alicia shows clearly that she knows what she is talking about and that she expects to make it make sense, both to herself and to her audience. She also shows that she knows how to approach that task in writing. She demonstrates her understanding that an effective piece of expository writing has a clear purpose (stated at the beginning and ending of this piece), supported with specific details and examples. No teacher was there to remind Alicia of this before she wrote. No models were available. There were no specific directions to follow. Instead, Alicia needed to transfer skills she had learned while writing informational pieces and responses to literature to an abstract, self-chosen task that was important to her. She made a plan and did exactly that, effectively explaining why Kristin deserved this award.

In Students' Voices

The letters to Mohammed Yunus asking him to continue the microloans for poor people in developing countries were written at the very end of the school year. After they were written, the teacher asked her students to read them aloud to each other. Sitting in a circle, students and teacher listened to and reflected on what each one had written. Afterwards, the teacher—wanting to hear from the students about their thinking—asked what about this independent writing task had been challenging for them.

Students responded enthusiastically and thoughtfully, with a range of comments about their work. Interestingly, not one of the sixth-, seventh-, and eighth-grade students in the class mentioned basic elements of writing. Nobody said, "Well, I wasn't quite sure how to set up a focus," or " I just couldn't figure out how to organize this."

When asked about this, one eighth-grade student spoke up, a bit impatiently, as if the teacher had asked her how she had figured out how to use her pencil. "Well," she said, "we've written pieces like this our *whole lives,* ever since we were little. We're always having to set up a focus and organize. We've written *zillions* of these pieces!"

The class nodded in assent. This seemed to ring true with everyone.

Over the course of the discussion, students spoke of various challenges. They mentioned having to be careful about being repetitious, about trying to figure out names for their characters, about making sure Mr. Yunus would be convinced. In diverse ways, they addressed the content of the piece, the effect of the microloan on a fictionalized recipient.

The words of one student were memorable. "I knew I was making up a character," he said. "But really, the whole point of this was to show something that was true. I needed to show the real effects of the microloans, even though I was making up this particular person. So, I had to—you know—keep thinking about what was *really true* about the microloans and figure out how they really would have affected this person. I couldn't just make stuff up."

Not all of the students produced such strong writing, but most produced workable pieces. The best news was not simply that the students had written effectively, however. Instead, what was notable was that they had both transferred the many pieces of their learning about writing to this new task and, even more so, that they could articulate what made it effective: *that what matters in writing is honest, thoughtful understanding, expressed clearly in a focused, organized, effective way.*

How did students acquire the ability to transfer what they knew about writing to a new situation? Did a miracle occur?

In a sense, of course, yes—learning *is* a miracle. But it is a miracle that we have some insight into. As the National Research Council reminds us, there is still much we do not know about how the brain learns. However, it is also true, as we saw at the beginning of this chapter, that there is much we do know about how transfer happens. Transfer can happen when students have deep initial learning. It can happen when students have plenty of opportunity, and time, to work with specific knowledge in specific contexts. Transfer can happen when students are helped to abstract under-lying principles from these specific contexts. Transfer can happen when students frequently have the experience of self-monitoring and getting and giving feedback.

Because of *Writing for Understanding*, all of these students have had those experiences. For them, transfer is a reality. Clearly, that transfer has many faces and can look quite different, depending on the age of the writer, the content he is working with, and the skills that he has been taught. However, what all of these varied pieces of writing have in common is this: each writer, at his or her appropriate developmental level, was able to construct meaning in an effective piece of writing. In a new context, each writer was able to make an overall internal plan for his thinking and writ-ing, monitor the work, and come up with a piece of writing that is effective and successful.

We can predict that all of these writers will approach their next tasks (provided they are appropriately planned and appropriately challenging) with a sense of, "I can do this. I am a thinker. I am a problem-solver. I am a writer. "

For teachers, that is music for the soul.

TO SUMMARIZE....

- **Research tells us that, in order to transfer knowledge and skills to new situations, students need adequate initial learning, plenty of practice, plenty of time devoted to that practice, a sense of abstraction of underlying principles, and the motivation to learn which often comes from previous success with a related task. *Writing for Understanding* builds all of these into writing instruction in a way that is both effective for students and manageable for teachers.**

- **When students are able to transfer their writing skills and expectation for meaning-making to new situations requiring writing, it is not because of a miracle of some sort; rather, it is because the conditions that lead to transfer have been met.**

Appendix A

The plan below is a part of a reading / writing / technology unit designed to help fifth graders develop comprehension strategies for nonfiction text and to write a focused report using the same text features that appear in published nonfiction text. Each student writes a report that demonstrates a thorough understanding of a woman who has made important contributions to the world, and which uses appropriate text features to enhance the text.

Writing for Understanding Sample Plan
Women in History

Central Ideas

What is it that I want students to understand about this content? What understandings about the craft of writing/reading do I want them to get?

- *Content:* Women have made significant contributions to our world and individual women have special qualities that helped them accomplish what they did.
- *Writing:* To write informational text effectively, we include appropriate facts and details that support a

focusing statement and exclude extraneous and inappropriate information.

- *Technology:* Text features, including those created using publishing software, enhance informational text.
- *Reading:* Readers use a variety of comprehension strategies to make sense of informational text.

Focusing Question

What question will I pose so that students can see how to approach this thinking and writing in a specific, appropriate, manageable way?

- What special qualities did the woman you studied have that helped her accomplish what she did?

Building and Processing Working Knowledge

How am I going to make sure that students know enough about this subject by the end to actually be able to write about it? How will they learn about the craft of writing?

- Teach/re-teach reciprocal teaching. Self-assess ability to use reciprocal teaching procedure and informational text comprehension strategies.
- Introduce assessment tool and benchmark pieces.
- Introduce note-taking options, set up note-taking pages in notebooks.
- Hear the teacher think aloud as she models the process of reading and note taking.
- Pairs of students read their text selections and take notes using reciprocal teaching.
- Written summaries of their notes.

- Infer qualities/attributes of famous women with supporting information from texts.
- Write a focusing statement that answers the focusing question.

Structure

How will students know how to build this piece of writing so that their thinking is clear, both to them as writers and to the readers of their work?

- Close read of some reports by last year's students with discussion.
- Review Painted Essay chart in the room and internal paragraph structural options.
- Remind students of the structures used in their "Responses to Text" in the fall.
- Model a report plan with a famous woman.
- Plan text features that enhance the report.

Writing

How will students draft and revise so that their final writing is clearly focused, organized, and developed to show understanding of the central ideas?

- Say the piece as they would like to write it, to another student/students.
- Self-assess notes for readiness to write.
- Write drafts in chunks: First an introduction with focusing statement. Check, go on.
- Write body paragraphs, check and have students self-assess against benchmark paragraphs.
- Instruction in paragraph construction options.
- Small guided writing groups as necessary.

- Conclusion Instruction/Lesson/Worksheet. Students learn options for conclusions that match their thinking. Complete the conclusions. Share.
- Use publishing software to format their reports.
- Self-assess with assessment tool from the beginning of the sequence.
- Orally share final draft of reports, answer questions and celebrate with families.

Appendix B

The plan below is a part of a unit designed to help fourth graders develop comprehension strategies for reading nonfiction text. After reading an article called "Caring for Your Pet Rat," each student writes a response to text that demonstrates a thorough understanding of the main idea of the article.

Writing for Understanding Sample Plan
Caring for Your Pet

Central Ideas

What is it that I want students to understand about this content? What understandings about the craft of writing do I want them to get?

- *Content:* Caring for pets requires attention to the needs of the pets.
- *Reading:* Effective readers synthesize information within a text.
- *Writing:* To show understanding, writers select and organize evidence to support a focus.

Focusing Question

What question will I pose so that students can see how to approach this thinking and writing in a specific, appropriate, manageable way?

How will they learn about the craft of writing?

According to the author, what are some important things you need to do to properly care for a pet rat?

Building and Processing Working Knowledge

How am I going to make sure that students know enough about this subject by the end to actually be able to write about it?

- Introduce focusing question: According to the author, what are some important things you need to do to properly care for a pet rat?
- Read the first half of the article "Caring for Your Pet Rat" together, modeling on the overhead how to highlight information that will help to answer the focusing question. Have students work in pairs to finish highlighting the article.
- Have each student draw a detailed, annotated diagram of a rat's cage, incorporating as much highlighted information from the text as possible.
- Prompt students to suggest categories that would help them to organize their information (food, housing, exercise, etc.).
- Instruct each student to choose two of these categories as headings for a prewriting chart. Guide each student in choosing appropriate information from the text to complete his/her own chart.

Structure

How will students know how to build this piece of writing so that their thinking is clear, both to them as writers and to the readers of their work?

Guide students in using a familiar structure (the Painted Essay) to color code and analyze a teacher-written model, "How to Care for Your Pet Dinosaur." Emphasize the way specific details are organized and elaborated to support the focus of the model.

Writing

How will students draft and revise so that their final writing is clearly focused, organized, and developed to show understanding of the central ideas?

Have students draft and revise their pieces "one paragraph at a time," stopping between paragraphs to share their work, get feedback, review the model, and discuss key elements.

Appendix C
***Writing for Understanding* Template**
(see next page)

Writing for Understanding Instruction
Teacher Plan

Teacher _____

Class_____ Date _____

Writing genre _____

Topic/Subject/Text

Central Ideas
What do I want students to understand about this content?
What understandings about the craft of writing do I want
them to develop?

Content:

Reading:

Writing:

Focusing Question
What question will I pose so
that students can see how
to approach this thinking
and writing in a specific,
appropriate, manageable way?

Focus (answer to
focusing question)

Building and Processing Working Knowledge

How will I make sure that students learn enough about this subject to actually be able to write about it?

- Vocabulary
- Guided reading
- Text mapping
- Paraphrasing
- Summarizing
- Visualizing
- Imaging
- Dramatizing
- Oral processing/ Guided conversation/ Think-pair-share
- Constructed response
- Experience
- Debating
- Taking notes (graphic organizers, T-charts, 2-column notes, etc.

Structures

How will students know how to organize their ideas and construct the piece of writing?

- Teacher-written models
- Teacher-and-student written models
- Various types of templates or frames (ex: Painted Essay)

Writing/Revising

How will students draft/revise so that their final writing is clearly focused, organized, and developed to show understanding of the central ideas?

- Group write, fully or in part

- Write section at a time

- Write full piece independently

- Revise/share full group

- Revise/share partners

- Proofreading in partners

- Proofread aloud, independently